GHOSTS OF THE
SOUTH CAROLINA
MIDLANDS

GHOSTS OF THE SOUTH CAROLINA MIDLANDS

TALLY JOHNSON

Haunted America

Published by Haunted America
A Division of The History Press
Charleston, SC 29403
www.historypress.net

Copyright © 2007 by Tally Johnson
All rights reserved

Cover image: original art by Marshall Hudson

First published 2007

Manufactured in the United Kingdom

ISBN 978.1.59629.200.0

Library of Congress Cataloging-in-Publication Data

Johnson, Talmadge.
Ghosts of the South Carolina midlands / Tally Johnson.
p. cm.
ISBN 978-1-59629-200-0 (alk. paper)
1. Ghosts--South Carolina. 2. Haunted places--South Carolina. 3. South Carolina--History. I. Title.
BF1472.U6J654 2007
133.109757'7--dc22

2007021482

CONTENTS

SOUTH CAROLINA TOURISM DISTRICTS COVERED IN THIS BOOK

Old 96 District Tourism Commission
204 East Public Square, P.O. Box 448
Laurens, South Carolina 29360
Phone: 1-800-849-9633
Fax: 1-864-984-0096
visitus@sctravelold96.com
Covers Abbeville, Edgefield, McCormick, Greenwood (and Laurens) Counties.

Thoroughbred Country
P.O. Box 850
Aiken, South Carolina 29802
Phone: 1-803-649-7981
Toll Free: 1-888-834-1654
tourism@lscog.org
Covers Aiken, Allendale, Bamberg and Barnwell Counties

Santee Cooper Country
Phone: 1-800-227-8510
http://www.santeecoopercountry.org/
Covers Orangeburg and Calhoun (and Berkeley, Clarendon and Sumter) Counties

Capital City and Lake Murray Country
P.O. Box 1783
Irmo, SC 29063
Phone: 1-866-SC JEWEL
http://lakemurraycountry.com/
Covers Lexington and Saluda (and Richland and Newberry) Counties

Contact any of these groups for more information on events, lodging and related matters.

ACKNOWLEDGEMENTS

To the public school teachers and media specialists of South Carolina, especially those at (the former) Lyman Elementary School, D.R. Hill Middle School, Dreher High School, James F. Byrnes High School, Midland Valley High School, South Carolina School for the Deaf and Blind, the Chester Park School of the Arts and Oakdale Elementary School. I appreciate everything you do and without your attention, commitment and concern, neither this book nor this author would be worth anything. To those at the schools I have not named directly, thank you for your example. Trust me, you have more positive influence than you'll ever know, and thanks for letting me come visit and hopefully help inspire some of your kids.

And to my wife, Rachel, I love you and thank you for your love, support and tolerance for this and all my other quirks.

And a very special mention to my younger brother, Brennan Johnson, and our dear friend Amy Ravenel.

INTRODUCTION

First, let me open this introduction by thanking those of you who bought my first book, *Ghosts of the South Carolina Upcountry*. I have heard from many of you and I want to thank you in print for your kind words. I always felt that there was a market for a well-written book of ghost lore featuring new material, and based on sales of the first book, I was correct. Since the first book was published, I have been asked the same questions over and over at book signings and storytelling appearances. Do you really believe in ghosts? Have you really had any of the experiences you describe in your book(s)? How did you manage to get published? And, how much do you make doing this? I'll answer these questions here, though I know I'll be asked again.

As far as my belief in ghosts is concerned, anywhere from one third to one half of all Americans believe in ghosts, so I'm hardly in the minority. Even discarding the evidence of my own senses and experiences, the fact that the belief in ghosts has been a part of civilization since the ancient Greeks, especially in literature, gives credence to the conviction that in certain circumstances, something may linger after death. Too many eyewitnesses have reported paranormal experiences for all of them to merely be written off. The fact that erstwhile ghost hunting groups have sprung up in every state of the union, in most countries and have gathered hard data throughout these hunts helps perpetuate this belief.

The primary reason I believe in ghosts though is simply what I have seen and otherwise experienced since my interest in the subject was first piqued. The stories told by myself and other eyewitnesses are too similar to be merely mass hysteria. Now, do I believe that ghosts are evil creatures hell-bent on harming the living, physically or otherwise? No, of course not. I'll leave that nonsense to the folks in Hollywood. As I often say during storytelling gigs at schools, no ghost has ever hurt me in any way. The shock of seeing one has caused me, or those with me, to react in a hazardous way, but the actual manifestation has had no impact on me. Most ghosts are simply reliving a part of their lives. For some, it is their last moments of life, and for others, just random parts of it. A few wish to pass on messages to the living in one form or another, while others believe they are still alive and continue with a daily routine. Most ghosts are tied to either a particular place or object and only appear if these are threatened in some way. I make no claims to having any psychic prowess or to having any ability to "lay" ghosts or send them to "the other side." I'm just an ordinary guy with a family and friends and a rather interesting hobby. I go "ghost seeking," a term that I like better than "hunting" or "busting." Ghost busting or ghost hunting imply capturing ghosts like animals for a zoo or getting rid of them like roaches. I firmly believe that most ghosts are like most people; they want to be left alone in familiar surroundings. If you need a ghost removed from a house, call a priest or a psychic of some kind, not me. If you want to experience something strange and fascinating, then call me. Heck, call me if you simply want me to entertain your group with some scary stories told with a hint of humor and a lack of seriousness. So finally, to answer your question, yes, Virginia, I really do believe in ghosts.

Both this book and *Ghosts of the South Carolina Upcountry* have featured my own personal experiences with the paranormal. Not in every case have I actually had an experience, but it happens often enough to bolster my belief in ghosts. Part of my attraction is that I try to be honest with my readers; if nothing happened to me at a location, despite the great legend attached to a place, I'll simply say so. Ghosts are not like movies in the sense that they do not appear on a regular schedule, and not everyone has the same experience. Many times I have been ghost seeking and had nothing out of the ordinary occur, while someone I was with saw an apparition or felt a cold spot. And, yes, at times the opposite has occurred. To some, this discrepancy helps explain away ghostly activity, since people in the same place at the same time should have similar experiences. To me, it helps prove the existence of paranormal activity. Not every birdwatcher sees the same birds during an expedition and no two stamp collectors have the same items in their collections. Why should ghosts be any different? Since the first book was published, I have had many people tell me that they had no idea such and such place was haunted, despite living in the area all their lives. I have also had folks tell me about numerous spots I missed for the first book. While others' experiences may differ, I have taken the word of interview subjects and, of course, myself to compile the facts.

INTRODUCTION

The story of how this book and *Ghosts of the South Carolina Upcountry* came to be is not one of long struggle and hard work finally paying off. I simply got lucky, which sometimes pays off just as much as hard work. I have been interested in ghosts for about a quarter century. Nancy Roberts, one of the premier storytellers and folklorists in the Carolinas, came to my elementary school when I was in the fifth grade. I remember sitting cross-legged on the floor listening in rapt fascination as she told us stories of the Gray Man, Theodosia Burr, the Hound of Goshen and others. As a longtime reader, I immediately cleaned out the Lyman library of every one of its books; well, the three they had anyway. When I saw the photographs of what I swore were real ghosts, I was hooked. Now that I know they were double exposures, I'm still impressed, but I am kind of disappointed. At any rate, I soon acquired library cards for all the surrounding counties and began my search for more new ghost stories. Thanks to parents who were tolerant of my newfound love of libraries and willing to drive me all over the place, I had read every book of ghost stories in about six counties by the time I started high school. Of course, my allowance and any money from chores, birthdays and Christmas went toward purchasing the ones I really liked. In high school, my friends and I would go ghost seeking about every weekend, except during football season; many of these trips appear in *Ghosts of the South Carolina Upcountry*. I steadily kept buying books of regional and national ghost lore up through college and continued going on ghost seeking expeditions with friends.

During my abortive attempt at completing my master's degree at Winthrop, I attempted to place some of the ghost lore I knew into historical context, only to be told that it was not a worthy topic for a thesis in history. After my marriage, my wife Rachel encouraged me to come tell ghost stories to her elementary school classes. For a child who had overcome a severe speech defect and near-terminal shyness, this was quite a change. As the number of storytelling gigs grew and the responses stayed positive, I noticed that the volumes of ghost lore I was buying all had the same tales in them and lacked sources and, in most cases, decent directions to the sites. After repeatedly griping about this, Rachel and some friends of ours told me that I should write the kind of ghost book I wanted to read. So I started pulling notes together and revisited some of my old stomping grounds. In the course of my duties as local history coordinator at the Chester County Library, I became active in PALMCOP (Palmetto Archives, Libraries and Museums Council on Preservation) and served on the organization's board. At a joint meeting of PALMCOP and the South Carolina Archival Association, a display from The History Press, based in Charleston, South Carolina, caught my eye. Among the books featured on their display was

Haunted Harbor by Geordie Buxton and Ed Macy. While chatting with the representative, I mentioned that I was working on a book of Upstate South Carolina ghost lore and asked if they might be interested. To my surprise, they were and agreed to publish it. Words cannot express the joy of seeing my name on a book at my local Books-A-Million. The History Press has since requested a second volume, and here it is, *Ghosts of the South Carolina Midlands*.

Concerning the final question about my earnings from these books—it's not enough. I won't be retiring to the tropics off my royalties anytime soon. So far I have made back my expenses and had a little left over. But money wasn't the reason for writing either of these books. I wrote them to share fascinating ghost stories with a wider audience. Now you don't have to be a native of Abbeville to hear about the lady in white at the Opera House or a native of Chester to hear about the haunting at the Chester Little Theater. I also wanted to put the ghost lore into a historical context, which is why I did a brief history of each county. I have included sources in both books to point out where additional information can be found for the various hauntings. I hope you enjoy reading this book as much as I enjoyed researching and writing it. Hopefully, it will inspire you to see for yourself if there is anything to these tales or to write your own book. Frankly, I hope it inspires you to buy a copy of *Ghosts of the South Carolina Upcountry*.

Author's Note: All accounts and events in this book are related as they occurred to the people involved. The author has sought to verify all personal accounts with other sources, but in some cases, that was not possible. The author also states that the events in this book are true to the best of his knowledge. Any location where the author failed to have an experience may still be haunted, but some people are luckier than others.

Please do not trespass or vandalize sites found in this book, or any other collection of ghost lore; you're committing a crime, not to mention making the jobs of serious researchers like myself that much harder. Enjoy the book, but do so responsibly.

ABBEVILLE COUNTY

A bbeville County is located on the western border of South Carolina. It is bordered by the state of Georgia and the South Carolina counties of Anderson, Greenville, Laurens, Greenwood and McCormick. Abbeville is one of the original counties of South Carolina, dating from the initial establishment of the county system in 1785. Remains of Native American sites have not been found in large numbers, but the area was at least a hunting ground for the Cherokee and other tribes and a focal point for conflict following the influx of white settlers after 1740. The area that now forms the county was part of the Ninety Six District of Revolutionary fame, though it later lost land to Greenwood and McCormick Counties when they were organized. The county was the site of seven Revolutionary War skirmishes, including the site of the Star Fort at Ninety Six, which is now in Greenwood County, and Long Cane, which is now in McCormick County. Ninety Six will be discussed in more detail in the Greenwood County chapter.

No Civil War encounters of note occurred in the county, but two key events did occur here. Abbeville County is known as the "cradle and grave of the Confederacy" because one of the earliest meetings in South Carolina calling for secession after the election of Lincoln was held here on November 22, 1860, hence the cradle. (However, Chesterfield County also claims this distinction.) The grave part of the phrase comes from the fact that the final council of war held by Jefferson Davis was convened at the Burt-Stark Mansion on Main Street in downtown Abbeville on May 2, 1865. At this meeting, Davis became convinced of the futility of continuing resistance to the Union armies. Other notable Abbeville County Civil War figures include Francis Wardlaw, the author of the South Carolina Ordinance of Secession, and J. Clark Allen, one of the first casualties of the Civil War, who died on Sullivan's Island in February 1861.

Abbeville County has made several political contributions as well, giving South Carolina one governor, Patrick Noble, who died in office, and three U.S. senators, Christie Benet, Frank B. Gary and Ashbury Latimer. The county has also given the nation a Speaker of the U.S. House, Langdon Cheves, who served from 1814–1815, and a Speaker pro tem of the U.S. House, Armistead Burt, who held that position in 1848. Sam J. Lee, the first African American to serve as Speaker of the South Carolina House in the 1870s was from Abbeville County. Other notables from Abbeville County include Major Thomas Howie, "the Major of St. Lo" of World War II, and John C. Calhoun, the only man to serve as vice-president for two presidents who were from different political parties. Calhoun also served in the U.S. House, the U.S. Senate and as U.S. secretary of state. Charlayne Hunter-Gault, an award-winning journalist and the first black female to attend the University of Georgia, was also an Abbeville County native. The county was also the birthplace of Abner Lipscomb, who served on the state supreme courts of both Alabama and Texas. Lipscomb was a law student of John C. Calhoun. Additionally, the town of Due West in Abbeville County is the home of Erskine College, founded in 1839 by the Associate Reformed Presbyterian Church, making it the oldest four-year church college in South Carolina. Erskine Caldwell, author of the novel *Tobacco Road*, briefly attended Erskine College before he was expelled.

On a more contemporary note, Mike McCurry, press secretary to former President Bill Clinton, is also a native of Abbeville, and the Abbeville County Library is home to one of the best collections of Native American ceramics and art in the Southeast United States. In 1990, the town of Abbeville served as a location for the shooting of the Julia Roberts film *Sleeping with the Enemy*.

Abbeville Opera House:
Lady in White Still Loves a Good Show

The Abbeville Opera House is one of the cultural gems of South Carolina. It has been listed on the National Register of Historic Places since the 1970s. The Opera House was dedicated on October 1, 1908, as was the county courthouse. A few months later, Thomas Dixon's play *The Clansman*, later inspiration for D.W. Griffith's epic silent film classic *Birth of a Nation*, was the venue's first show, and it opened to rave reviews. The building hosted all the greats of vaudeville, including Jimmy Durante, the Ziegfeld Follies, Sarah Bernhardt and several traveling road shows. By the 1920s, silent films had largely replaced vaudeville and the Opera House became a movie theater, though the stage was left intact. The Opera House remained a movie theater until the late 1950s. In 1968, the Abbeville Community Theatre decided to restore the building to its original purpose as a home for plays. The rear wall of the building is one of the tallest free-standing brick walls in the state. The wall is eighteen inches thick from top to bottom and is built entirely of handmade brick; no steel beams or timber framing holds the wall in place. The rear wall was once the scene of a stunt by the famous magician Harry Houdini. He was handcuffed, bound with ropes, placed in a straitjacket and suspended from the roof in front of the sheer face of the rear wall. Naturally, he escaped with minimal difficulty. However, the best-known feature of the Abbeville Opera House is its ghost.

The haunting at the opera house has two very different versions. The first is found on several different websites. It centers on a lone chair located in the second balcony, which is where the figure of a young lady has been seen. The fact that the upper balcony was formerly the seating for black patrons has allowed speculation to flourish that the ghost is the victim of a racially motivated crime. However, according to this version, no crime has occurred that can be linked to the sightings of an apparition or any other paranormal activity involving the chair. The only known violent death in this area of the building was the shooting of a black suspect who escaped from the custody of the sheriff around 1915. The black male ran through the lobby and lower balcony of the opera house, only to meet his pursuer just outside the exit. Notice the suspect ran through the lower balcony and never entered the upper balcony.

The second and more likely version is easily obtained simply by contacting the executive director of the Abbeville Opera House, Michael Genevie. He explains that the second balcony has been cleared of all furniture except for one chair, as in the other version. However, he claims that following a successful performance, during the standing ovation the figure of a white lady dressed in a white Edwardian-era gown rises from that chair and joins the living audience below in showing her appreciation for a job well done. Of course the upper balcony was cleared of all other furniture at the request of the fire marshal shortly after the reopening of the building, and for this same reason, no one living is allowed on the second balcony during rehearsals and shows. No one currently connected to the opera house knows of any unattended lady who died in the building, and the literature on the site also mentions no deaths. Mr. Genevie has not seen or heard the ghost himself, but people he trusts have.

Sadly, I have not been able as yet to secure seats at any performances at the Abbeville Opera House nor has my schedule permitted me to take part in any ghost hunts or tours of the building. Hopefully I will be able to rectify this shortcoming soon. However, I am inclined to give credence to the second account of this haunting as many other theaters both in America and Britain have "lucky" ghosts as well. "Lucky" ghosts generally appear during rehearsals of plays destined to be hits at a certain venue. One of the best-known examples of this phenomenon is the Man in Gray at the Theatre Royal on Drury Lane in London. The Man in Gray has a knack for appearing in the balcony both during rehearsals and matinees of shows fated to be successful. He also has offered assistance of a kind to struggling actors at times. He is thought to be Joe Grimaldi, a comedian and singer who assisted up-and-comers, often offering them jobs in his plays or giving advice on timing or positioning before his death in 1837. Like his ghostly counterpart in western South Carolina, witnesses usually think he is either an eccentric or in costume until he vanishes from plain sight.

THE BELMONT INN:
NOT ALL GUESTS CHECK OUT BY 11 A.M.

The Belmont Inn is located across the street from the Abbeville Opera House and is sometimes thought to be the true home of the Lady in White mentioned above. It opened in 1903 as the Eureka and served as an overnight rest stop for railroad passengers and for actors playing at the Opera House. The Belmont Inn is on the National Register of Historical Places. It is also one of the most haunted hotels in inland South Carolina. At least two ghosts have been seen in the building and several other odd events have been reported to the owners.

One of the ghosts is known as Abraham and has been seen on the ground floor, though never for long. In fact, Alan Peterson, one of the current owners, says that Abraham mainly appears as a flicker of motion in the corner of the eye. The other ghost, a Scotsman, has been seen on the main stairs. How it was determined that the ghost is a Scot still puzzles me, but I will take the witnesses at their word. Many guests in different rooms have reported hearing knocks on their doors at odd hours, only to find no one there and no sign of anyone having passed by recently. Mr. Peterson told me that some minor poltergeist activity has been reported over the years. This activity is limited to staff members having small objects moved or misplaced and the occasional glass being broken while untouched by human hands. I did not have a chance to ask Mr. Peterson how often these events occur while preteen females are nearby. As far as poltergeists are concerned, I favor the theory that poltergeists are the tangible manifestation of female puberty or related stress. The two appear together in literature too frequently for this to be solely coincidence. However, I am only a ghost storyteller, not a trained parapsychologist, so my theory is worth about what anyone else's is.

I visited the Belmont Inn briefly while working on this book; however, I did not introduce myself as an author of ghost stories and claimed to be solely interested in reading the clippings on the lobby walls. I was of course hoping to see either the Scotsman on the stairs or catch a brief glimpse of Abraham. Sadly, I was not graced with their presence, though the building is a fascinating place and deserves a ghost even if I haven't met him yet.

ABBEWOOD BED AND BREAKFAST: GONE? MAYBE…

The Abbewood Bed and Breakfast is located near the Burt-Stark Mansion of Civil War fame. However, this beautiful bed and breakfast with a circular porch is better known for its ghost. The home was built about 1900 by J.R. Norwood. Mr. Norwood died of natural causes on the stairs of his home. When the current owners, Mr. and Mrs. Charlie Freeman, acquired the house and began some needed renovations, odd events soon followed as they often do in paranormal cases. Footsteps were heard upstairs at a point about halfway down the main staircase. While footsteps in a deserted hallway could be explained away, the second odd event, the smell of rotting flesh, was more difficult. The Freemans tried to locate any carrion in the attic or walls, but found nothing. A sympathetic friend suggested an exorcism just to put the Freemans' minds at ease. The Freemans grudgingly decided to try it, and to date the smell is no longer present and the footsteps have faded as well. Mr. Freeman did admit during our conversation that the usual noises found in old houses are still heard but so far so good on anything unusual. I would recommend a visit to check behind the Freemans. Sometimes things come back and maybe you'll get lucky.

ERSKINE COLLEGE: AN EXAMPLE OF WHY POLITICS DOESN'T MAKE GOOD COCKTAIL CONVERSATION

Erskine College—named for Ebenezer Erskine, one of the founders of The Associate Reformed Presbyterian Church—may be the oldest four-year religious college in South Carolina, but its haunted history almost belies that fact. I had to resort to a thirty-five-year-old document to find any evidence of paranormal events on campus. I am almost led to believe that Presbyterians are either better behaved than most religions or less inclined to believe in ghosts and such, but I retain my doubts due to the fact that I am one by marriage, and obviously I believe in ghosts. However, the story should be told. According to Grier's *Legends of Erskine*, in 1843 a debate on conditions in Cuba if Spanish rule were to end led to harsh words and manslaughter, if not murder. The debate was between members of the Euphemian and Philomathean Societies in the Old Main building on the Erskine campus in a room both societies shared on the second floor. Peter Thompson was rather strident in his opinion, and words were exchanged in the hallway outside the room after the end of the heated discussion. A scuffle broke out and a knife blade flashed shortly thereafter. Mister Thompson had his throat slit almost ear to ear. He died while being carried downstairs to summon medical help. The detail that pertains to us today is the fact that his blood stained the hallway for almost fifty years.

Sadly, I cannot confirm or deny the existence of the bloodstain today, since Old Main burnt to the ground in 1892, taking the bloodstain with it. However, I am inclined to accept the truth of the tale due to the prevalence of this type of haunting in other places; eternal bloodstains are found all over the world in many different settings, such as private homes, restaurants, churches and hotels.

OTHER ABBEVILLE SITES…FROM THE CHAMBER OF COMMERCE, OF ALL PLACES

The Chamber of Commerce headquarters is haunted according to Sheri Standridge, the director, who has reported lighting problems in the building. Besides the usual lights cutting on and off without manual help, electrical shorts and other issues have popped up with above average frequency. Her husband told her that a male voice once answered the phone while the building was empty. At the time, she was the only employee and was at another engagement. Other Abbeville County haunts include Trinity Episcopal Church—a lady named Elizabeth, who died at the time of the Civil War, is buried in the church cemetery and has been both seen and heard inside the sanctuary—and The Historical Society Museum located in the Old Jail (designed by Robert Mills, designer of the Washington Monument) where footsteps and odd noises, especially creaking noises coming from the third floor, have been heard. What makes this especially interesting is that the third floor was the location for the gallows. The Bundy-McCowan-Barksdale House is also the site of a ghost taking a stroll, as the footsteps are heard but no accompanying body is ever seen.

AIKEN COUNTY

Aiken County was formed in 1871 from parts of Barnwell, Edgefield, Lexington and Orangeburg Counties. It is the only county in South Carolina that was founded by the "Reconstruction" Legislature. It is bordered by the State of Georgia and Edgefield, Saluda, Lexington, Orangeburg and Barnwell Counties. Aiken County was named for William Aiken, the President of the South Carolina Canal and Railroad Company and a leader in the early industrial development of the county. Native American settlement in the area predates the passing of the Spanish under the command of Hernando de Soto at Beech Island in 1539. De Soto robbed the natives, both living and dead, at the town of Port Comfort (near the Savannah River Site) during his visit. He was angry about the lack of silver in the area. He and his troops kidnapped the queen of the town, Cacique, and stole fourteen bushels of freshwater pearls after finding the body of de Soto's brother. The area was the site of several trading posts prior to 1760, when permanent white settlement began. The dominant tribe was the Creeks, though the Cherokees and Tuscaroras have also left some remains in the area. The tensions over English settlement came to a head in 1764 with several raids in the area by the Creeks. Following the defeat of the tribes, the Creeks left the area for modern Alabama.

In 1776, Aiken County was visited by Pioneer botanist William Bartram when he passed through the area on his four-year journey through the southern colonies. The county was also the site of three Revolutionary skirmishes, and the northern terminus of the first railway in South Carolina (at completion in 1832, the world's longest at 136 miles) was at the river port of Hamburg, now abandoned and near modern North Augusta.

At the end of the Civil War, Aiken was the site of a cavalry skirmish known as the Battle of Aiken, which we will discuss in greater detail shortly. After 1876, the area became known as a popular winter resort for wealthy Northerners. The reputation Aiken County has attained in the tennis, polo and horse racing worlds dates from this period. This prestigious reputation occurred despite Aiken being the birthplace of the "Red Shirts" featured in Wade Hampton's successful campaign for the governor's chair during the "Redemption" campaign of 1876. For those who may have slept through South Carolina history, the "Red Shirts" were former Confederate officers who formed private rifle clubs in order to train men to support Hampton in the election by any means necessary. The election of 1876 was known as the "Redemption" as it led to the end of Republican rule in the state and the reemergence of white supremacy. The town of Hamburg was the site of an armed clash between whites and blacks that helped the election of Hampton and ended any hopes of the formation of a biracial reform party in the Reconstruction era.

Well-known Congresspersons from the Aiken area include Robert C. DeLarge, African American member of Congress from the Charleston area from 1871–1873, and Willa Fulmer, widow of longtime Congressman H.P. Fulmer who replaced him in Congress from 1944–45, both born in Aiken. In 1931, Nicolas Longworth, Speaker of the U.S. House of Representatives and son-in-law of U.S. President Theodore Roosevelt, died in Aiken while visiting friends. The only U.S. senator and South Carolina governor from Aiken County was James Henry Hammond, who famously declared in a speech to the U.S. Senate, "Cotton is king!" His home, Redcliffe near Beech Island, will be the subject of a section as well.

Other famous people with ties to the present Aiken County include Thomas Hitchcock Jr., a champion polo player and fighter pilot in both World Wars; John S. Billings, first editor of *Life* magazine; and Dwight Davis, three-time men's doubles champion at Wimbledon, founder of the Davis Cup international tennis competition and U.S. secretary of war under President Calvin Coolidge. Davis had a winter home in the area. Confederate Brigadier General Gabriel Rains, reputed inventor of the torpedo, is buried at Saint Thaddeus Episcopal Church. Biblical scholar and author Louis Cassels lived in Aiken. Among his works are *The Real Jesus* and *Your Bible*. Henry Ravenal, mycologist and diarist was born in Aiken. One of the first female holders of a Doctor of Medicine degree, Jane Guignard, was born in the county as was William "Hootie" Johnson, former chairman of the Augusta National Golf Club. Noted children's book author Idella Bodie now lives in Aiken, and Marie Seigler, the founder of the Aiken County Girls Tomato Club—forerunner to the modern 4-H clubs, was a native of the county as well. Ellen Axson, later first wife of President Woodrow Wilson was baptized at All Saints' Episcopal Church in Aiken. Brothers Michael Dean and William "The Refrigerator" Perry, who were both All-Pro defensive linemen in the National Football League for the Cleveland Browns and Chicago Bears (among others) respectively and All-Americans at Clemson University. The brothers are Aiken natives as well.

A good-sized portion of the county is part of the U.S. government's Savannah River Site. A branch campus of the University of South Carolina, USC-Aiken, is located in the county as well. Among the notable area attractions is Hitchcock Woods, home of the Blessing of the Hounds, which occurs every Thanksgiving. Hitchcock Woods includes the largest urban forest reserves in the South and was the site of the first outdoor polo match in the United States. Other attractions include the Thoroughbred Hall of Fame and Hopeland Gardens, which features a "touch and smell" trail for the visually impaired. Local festivals include the Chitlin Strut in Salley, the Jack O' Lantern Jubilee in North Augusta and the Sassafras Festival in Burnettown.

ANNIE'S INN:
SHE STILL WANTS "MAMA"

Annie's Inn is located in the Montmorenci community. It is one of the better known bed and breakfasts in Aiken County and is popular year-round. It is also home to one of the best known ghost tales to come from Aiken County. The most common attribute of the haunting here is the figure of a little girl in nineteenth-century dress who can be heard calling for "Mama." Sometimes she is seen and not heard and at times the opposite occurs. The focal point of this haunting is the main staircase, though the girl has been seen outside on the grounds as well. No deaths have been reported, but given that the house is over a century old and the high rate of childhood mortality at the time, this reappearance is not surprising. What came as a shock to both the owner, Scottie Ruark, and the manager, Diana Williams, was the guest who asked if the house was haunted, but not for the same reason. The guest reported that she had seen a male figure upstairs. To date, she is the only person to see this man, so you may be next. Opinion at Annie's Inn is that the man and the girl are probably father and daughter. In addition to these two apparitions, disembodied footsteps have been heard on the stairs and in the upstairs hallway, and figures have been seen "from the corner of your eye" all over the building.

On my one visit to Annie's Inn, I did not encounter anything unusual, but I eagerly await the chance to get back down and attempt to connect the man and the girl in some way. If I see either or both, then it will be not just a good trip, but a great one.

ROSEMARY HALL:
MRS. JACKSON STILL LOOKS AFTER THINGS

Rosemary Hall was built in 1902 by the founder of the town of North Augusta, James U. Jackson, as his home. It is on the National Register of Historical Places and is now an inn. According to multiple accounts, it is haunted by Mr. Jackson's wife who has been seen walking up and down the main staircase. The fact that her portrait hangs upstairs greatly aids in identification. Mrs. Jackson is also seen in room 205. She is usually wearing a shawl. That room has more than its share of television issues, especially with channels changing and the set powering on and off when the room is empty. Poltergeist activity has been reported, especially small items vanishing without cause only to pop up later in odd spots.

My visit to Rosemary Hall did not produce anything especially out of the ordinary except for hearing what I swear were footsteps in the lobby when I was alone and standing still. I highly recommend a visit, especially an overnight stay. Too many witnesses have reported similar occurrences for Rosemary Hall not to have a ghost or two.

REDCLIFFE PLANTATION:
HISTORY, HAGS AND HAUNTED...WHAT A PACKAGE

Beech Island is one of the most historic sites in South Carolina. It was a major Native American trade center up to and even after de Soto's disastrous social call and up until the Revolution. About 1840, the island was acquired by the Hammond family and has since served as a monument to the family's long and distinguished service to both state and nation. Several different stories have gathered around this site.

The most far-fetched was reported to the Works Progress Administration (WPA) by a former slave, who I personally believe would have been owned by the Hammond family. The story concerns a woman who could unroll her skin and go cavorting as a hag (witch). Her husband found her discarded skin and put salt and pepper in and on it. When she returned, she was stunned that she could not reenter her skin and fled. To date, no one has reported any encounters with either the husband or wife.

Another story at Beech Island begins at Redcliffe Plantation where three trees in front of the building emanate a deep feeling of unease that lingers in the area as long as you do. Inside the house, a shadowy figure is sometimes seen staring at passersby and on occasion touching them. Governor and Senator James Henry Hammond has been seen pacing the halls as well. Unfounded rumors of incest and other slurs dogged Hammond's political career and may explain why he returns seeking peace of mind and a degree of vindication. The defeat of the South and the decline of the "cotton kingdom" may play a role as well. Hammond's great-grandson, John Shaw Billings, has been heard typing on an old manual typewriter in the library.

Naturally, I have not seen any trace of the hag, nor has anyone else to my knowledge. On a visit to Redcliffe in college while studying James Henry Hammond, I toured the house and felt the unease caused by the unusual arrangement of trees in front of the house, but sadly, I have not yet seen Senator Hammond.

BATTLE OF AIKEN: ROBERT E. LEE WASN'T THERE THEN, BUT NOW?

The Battle of Aiken was one of the few bits of good news to reach Confederate ears from the time when Sherman left Savannah until after the burning of Columbia. It was a classic cavalry battle that was fought to protect Augusta—one of the few river ports still usable by the Confederacy—and the cottons mills at Graniteville. The Union cavalry was commanded by Major General Judson Kilpatrick who had recently burned Barnwell before seizing and destroying the railroad tracks and several cars near Blackville. Kilpatrick was unpopular with civilians because he refused to control his foragers, better known as bummers. Many complaints of rape and general ill-treatment followed Kilpatrick through South Carolina. He was also known as "Kill-Cavalry" due to his poor tactics and lack of concern for the welfare of his men.

The Confederate cavalry was led by Joseph Wheeler, known as "Fighting Joe," who ranked just behind J.E.B. Stuart and Wade Hampton in his skills as a cavalry leader. Wheeler decided to intercept Kilpatrick in Aiken on February 10, 1865. He set up an ambush in town and ordered his men to hold their fire until all of Kilpatrick's men were in range. Of course, a few troopers opened fire prematurely, springing the trap early. At the end of the melee, which featured hand-to-hand combat and flashing sabers, the Confederates held the field and had blunted Sherman's feint toward Augusta. General Kilpatrick fled the field ahead of a handful of Confederate troopers, losing his hat in his rush to escape. Union losses (killed, wounded and captured) were 495. Confederate losses (killed, wounded and captured) were 251. Of course, Sherman completely bypassed the Augusta area after the skirmish and pressed on to Columbia, Cheraw and Bentonville.

On February 10–13 every year, the E. Porter Alexander Camp of the Sons of Confederate Veterans hosts a reenactment of the battle. One feature of this reenactment is a cavalry charge including a few riderless horses to honor the fallen. At the 1999 reenactment, a photojournalist documenting the scene took a photograph that shows a Confederate general, who was far from the field of battle in February 1865, riding one of the horses. According to an account published by Randall Floyd, noted Southern folklorist, when the photograph was developed General Robert E. Lee was seen on one of the riderless horses. Several experts examined the photograph and declared it genuine. Sadly, no reenactments since have been marked by any other ghostly activity.

I have not been lucky enough to see the photograph or any reproductions of it. However, I seriously doubt that General Lee even gave any thought to the Battle of Aiken either at the time it occurred or in the remaining five years he lived afterward. I imagine he would have been more concerned with the immediate aftereffects of the fall of Richmond and the approaching Union army under General Grant. The fact that General Lee does not reappear at his former home in Arlington, Virginia, or at any other Civil War battlefield, like Gettysburg, Petersburg or even Appomattox, leads me to believe that the general has found lasting peace. Also, most ghosts tend to have some connection to a site they return to, however fleeting. I have found no tie between General Lee and the Aiken area. In Mr. Floyd's article on the photograph, he states that there is a strong resemblance to other well-known photos of General Lee on horseback as seen in works by noted Civil War scholars like Emory Thomas, which only gives credence to my personal theory that the photograph is an accidental double exposure. My one time witnessing the reenactment was an enjoyable and educational experience, but I have no unusual happenings to report.

MIDLAND VALLEY'S OWN PHANTOM HITCHHIKER: HECK OF A WAY TO AVOID A HONEYMOON

S.C. Highway 421 between Aiken and Augusta lies on the original route of U.S. Highway 1. The road runs fairly straight and at first glance is not much different from thousands of miles of roads all over the country. However, if the article I found in the *Aiken Standard* newspaper and my own experiences are to be believed, it has a rather sad tale to tell. According to local lore, a young couple from North Carolina stopped in Aiken to get married before continuing on to Florida in the early 1920s. The weather turned stormy just after the ceremony. Not far from the community of Steifeltown, their car ran out of gas. Luckily for the newlyweds, a local was driving by and offered to take one of them to get a can of gas. The groom decided to stay with the car and their bags, so the young bride went to get the gas. The bride and her good Samaritan found an open gas station at the hamlet of Schultz Hill and were en route back to the probably impatiently waiting groom when the slick road intervened. The driver and his lovely passenger were both killed when he lost control of the car near the community of Burnettown, about halfway between Schultz Hill and Steifeltown. After this devastation, the groom was seen bouncing from bar to bar along the highway until he faded from history. However, drivers on Highway 421 have reported seeing the young bride in her gown hitching a ride on rainy nights. A few unfortunates have picked her up, only to hear her gut-wrenching scream and see her vanish from the front seat.

I have only driven on S.C. Highway 421 once, and the weather was clear and the sun high in the sky. However, my father has driven that route while visiting my aunt and uncle in North Augusta, and he told me that one rainy evening about 7:00 p.m. he saw what he thought was a young lady in a white formal gown walking on the shoulder. He did not pick her up, as his car was a bit more cluttered than usual. He mentioned that after he passed her he glanced in the rear view mirror and no one was there. He assumed that either someone else had picked her up or she had arrived at her destination. He did say that he thought the nearest intersection was Richardson Lake Road and Highway 421, which corroborates reports that she usually vanishes near that intersection.

GRANITEVILLE:
HISTORIC AND HAUNTED

The community of Graniteville in central Aiken County was founded in 1845 by William Gregg. It was the site of the first cotton mill in the South and the first compulsory education system in the South, as workers were fined if their children did not attend school. It was also the location of a tragic train wreck in 2005, when a failed switch caused a moving freight train to collide with a parked train on a spur track near one of the mills.

Nine people died from chlorine inhalation, and the resulting cleanup costs forced the mill's owner, Avondale Mills, to close.

Prior to this most recent tragedy, the late 1800s witnessed an event that haunts the nightmares of every parent with a small child under a sitter's care. Somewhere between the hill on which Graniteville Mill stood and the community of Madison, a mill hand left his baby in the care of a neighbor girl while he went to work his shift. This particular evening, a nasty storm was brewing that would leave weeping in its wake. The infant was frightened by the storm and kept up a steady distress signal for hours. Finally, the sitter, desperate for peace, grabbed a scarf and wrapped it around the baby's head. Naturally, the baby died of strangulation. On his return home, the father saw the sitter being led away by the authorities. He ran into his house and grabbed a pistol. In a few seconds, the girl fell to the ground pierced by multiple bullets. With her last breath, she waved the bloody scarf at the father and promised to return. On stormy nights her white-clad form has been seen walking along S.C. Highway 191 waving the bloody murder weapon.

I have not had a chance to seek out the truth of this legend, having discovered it as this book was in its final stages. But I hope to visit the area and attempt to verify that the girl still walks. I truly hope that the bride that walks on Highway 421 has not been confused with this murderous girl. Hopefully, a return visit will clarify things.

CALL IT THE HOTEL AIKEN, HOLLEY HOUSE OR THE COMMERCIAL HOTEL; JUST CALL IT HAUNTED, TOO

The Hotel Aiken has been a fixture of downtown Aiken for over one hundred years. It was built by Henry Hahn in 1898 to serve Northern tourists and salesmen and boasted fifty guestrooms with private baths, which was still a rarity in the South at the time. The Holley family acquired the hotel in 1929 and it stayed in the family until 2001, hence the name the Holley House. In the 1970s, the hotel was expanded and thirty rooms were added. Under the Holley family's ownership, the hotel became popular with both players and fans of the Masters Golf Tournament, played in nearby Augusta, Georgia, as well as with the horse and polo sets that frequent the Aiken area. The building also features a hand-operated service elevator, which some people believe is the oldest one still operating in South Carolina. The Hotel Aiken was returned to its original name when it was sold to Kishan Shah in 2001.

According to a variety of sources, the Hotel Aiken has more than a few guests who may have overstayed their welcome. Guests and employees alike have reported many curious events, especially on the second floor. Shadows that flit past on walls without reason, whispers in empty halls and the sounds of a woman either screaming or weeping are just a few. Locked doors in empty rooms open and close and toilets have been known to flush spontaneously as well. Housekeeping carts are found at the opposite end of the hall when employees emerge from cleaning a room. Room 225 seems to be a special focus. The television in that room is often found on even when no guests are present. The current owner, Kishan Shah, told me that he has not had any odd experiences, but believes that with a history as long as the building has, anything is possible. I myself have visited the Hotel Aiken briefly but did not gain access to the second floor, and although I experienced nothing strange, the reports are too varied for there not to be something to them.

ALLENDALE COUNTY

Allendale County was formed in 1919 from Barnwell and Hampton Counties. It is the newest county in South Carolina. Allendale County is bordered by Barnwell, Bamberg and Hampton Counties as well as the state of Georgia. The county was named for the town of Allendale, which was settled about 1840 and incorporated in 1878. The town itself was named for Paul Allen, the first postmaster. The discovery of chert quarries—which supplied material for blades and possibly for fire starting material—at sites in Allendale County show that humans with at least a Stone Age–level culture were in South Carolina by 10,000 BC. Native American settlement in the area dates to 2500 BC with key remains being flint quarries and mounds. Tribes found in the area included the Yamasee, Coosa and the Cherokee. The area was also the site of several raids by the Yamasee, Cherokee and Creek tribes prior to the Revolution. Two Revolutionary War skirmishes were fought in the county. During the Civil War, Sherman's troops passed through the area but no skirmishes resulted, which is not to say that the future county escaped unharmed. The original building of the Great Salkehatchie Baptist Church in Ulmer was destroyed in order to provide material to build bridges for the invaders.

Prominent figures of the county include well-known artist Jasper Johns who spent his childhood here. Although Allendale County has not yet given South Carolina a U.S. Senator, South Carolina Governor Robert McNair has called the county home. McNair was governor at the time of the Orangeburg Massacre. He also announced that the state would obey any federal court orders concerning school desegregation; he oversaw the first reapportionment of the South Carolina Senate in many years; and he was in office when women received the right to be called as jurors in 1966. Emmy winner Vertamae Grosvenor, author of *Travel Notes of a Geechee Girl* and frequent contributor to both National Public Radio and public television, was born in Allendale County.

JUST SLIPPED THIS ONE IN

This story made the book at almost literally the last second. I had been working on this book for about three months and had had no luck finding any ghostly legends from Allendale County at all. Out of desperation, I decided to return to the area for one last try at shaking something loose. I visited the Allendale County Library and their collection offered no help. I decided to just ride around in hopes of coming up with a plan B when, as so often happens, I stumbled upon one. I was driving home up S.C. Highway 641 (also known as the Confederate Highway) toward U.S. Highway 321 when I saw a road sign for Priesters Mill Road. Intrigued, I turned off in hopes of finding a mill that ran without human assistance or a headless Confederate sentry or anything extraordinary. Just as I approached the bridge over what I later found out was Jackson Branch, my iPod slid between the seats of the car. Already frustrated, I glanced in the rear view mirror and stopped to dig it out. As it was a fairly warm fall evening I had the windows down as I drove, and since the iPod had popped loose from the wire connecting it to my stereo, I was immediately struck by the silence of a country night. At least until I heard the unmistakable scream of a very upset baby. I have found no story explaining this event and it may have been wishful thinking; but I assure you, by that point my main focus was on arriving back home in Chester without hitting a deer en route. Hopefully, you will find the bridge and have a similar experience.

BAMBERG COUNTY

Bamberg County was formed in 1897 from Barnwell County. The county was named for William S. Bamberg, a major landowner in the area. It is bordered by Barnwell, Allendale, Hampton, Colleton and Orangeburg Counties. Native American activity in the area began with the Yamasee tribe before 1000 BC and was continued by various tribes until Cherokee raids in the area during the Cherokee War of 1760–61. The area that later became Bamberg County was not a hotbed of activity during the Revolution with no recorded military activity in the area. No U.S. senators or South Carolina governors have come from the county as yet. The only Civil War encounter of note occurred at Rivers Bridge near Ehrhardt. (We will discuss this battle in greater detail shortly.)

The inventors of the first submarine spar torpedo, Dr. Francis Carroll and his slave Louis, are natives of Bamberg County. Bamberg County is also the home of Voorhees College in Denmark and a satellite campus of the University of South Carolina, USC-Salkehatchie. Denmark is best known as the site of American Telegraph and Telephone's first transcontinental hub and was the site of connection for the first transcontinental telephone call. On January 15, 1885, the home of AT&T's president at Jekyll Island, Georgia, was connected to President Chester Arthur at the White House in Washington, D.C., who was also connected to Alexander Graham Bell in New York City and to Thomas Watson in San Francisco. Famous residents of Bamberg County include printmaker and artist, Jim Harrison; antebellum author and poet, William Gilmore Simms; and New York Mets 1986 World Series hero, William H. "Mookie" Wilson. Another well-known native of Bamberg County is Cleveland Sellers, the only person ever charged with a crime in connection with the Orangeburg Massacre. Sellers is currently head of the African American Studies program at the University of South Carolina. The best-known festival in the county is the Schtzenfest held in Ehrhardt. This is a shooting contest held to recognize the German heritage of the original settlers in the area. Denmark is also home to the Dogwood Festival.

RIVERS BRIDGE:
THINGS POP UP ALL THE TIME

The Battle of Rivers Bridge was the first organized attempt by Confederate troops to slow Sherman's advance through southeastern Georgia and western South Carolina after the fall of Savannah. Confederate Major General Lafayette McLaws led about 1,200 well-fortified troops who were blocking the crossing of the Salkehatchie River. Between the trenches and the heavy winter floods, McLaws felt secure and believed he could stall Sherman long enough for troops to rally behind him. On February 3, 1865, the Union right wing under Major General Francis P. Blair, totaling some 5,000 troops, decided to either overwhelm or outflank the obstructing Confederates. Hasty bridges were thrown up in the face of fairly steady artillery fire. Most of the Union infantry had to wade through chest-deep, freezing waters. Two Union brigades flanked the Confederates on their right and McLaws withdrew toward Branchville. Total casualties were about 300 with the Confederates losing the majority. The entire affray lasted a few hours and delayed Sherman for about a day.

In August 2006, I visited Rivers Bridge State Historic Site while doing research for this book. I needed a break from driving and the brochure for the park offered the promise of a one-and-a-half-mile interpretive trail. Since my real job concerns South Carolina history, I am ashamed to admit that this was my first visit to Rivers Bridge. I was aware of its role in the Civil War, but beyond that, I was simply after a few minutes of leg stretching. I paid the admission fee and took off down the trail. It took me a few minutes to get used to the quiet of the woods and surrounding marsh. Six hours of road noise and a very loud iPod didn't help to speed the transition. The markers were informative and the Confederate earthworks were well-preserved. I arrived at the river, where the trail turned to the right after about ten minutes, and decided to just stand there and see if I could add any birds to my life list, such as it is, or see any other wildlife. Black water rivers are a rare sight in the rolling hills of my native Upcountry, and as I stood there looking across the river, a flash of blue caught my eye just above the water line in the trees of the marsh. Thankfully I was alone, so I just stood still and quietly waited to see what it was. The blue moved out from behind a tree and I realized with a start that it was a dark-haired, bearded man in what appeared to be a blue wool jacket. He was carrying an old-fashioned rifle. I am not an expert on Civil War weapons, so forgive me if I plead ignorance as to what kind exactly it was. I thought about shouting a warning about swimming being prohibited, or even about snakes, but the shock of seeing him hit me like a shot. In amazement, I watched the figure, ignoring the steady buzz of feasting mosquitoes. When he thrust his arms out and fell backward into the murky water without a splash, the spell of the moment was broken. I was stunned to see anything out of the ordinary as no folklore is connected with the site. The fact that the battle was in February and my visit was in August also made the appearance of the apparition unexpected. I skipped the rest of the trail and decided to head back toward civilization. At the gate, I met a young couple from Tennessee who were Civil War buffs and working in the area. I explained the significance of the site to them briefly and headed toward Denmark. En route, I called my wife and told her about what I had seen. She humored me as wives often do their eccentric husbands.

Voorhees College:
Yet More Odd Goings-On on Campus

Voorhees College was founded by Elizabeth E. Wright and opened on April 14, 1897. Ms. Wright was a twenty-four-year-old graduate of the famed Tuskegee Industrial School founded by the noted African American educator Booker T. Washington. Despite poor health, she decided to follow in his footsteps and founded a school to provide industrial training to African Americans in South Carolina. After three failed attempts, she found a site in Denmark and the school began as the Denmark Industrial School. In 1902, the name was changed to honor Ralph Voorhees, a blind philanthropist who had provided both moral and financial aid to Wright and the school. Ms. Wright died at age thirty-four, just after her marriage.

According to a conversation I had with a security guard (who wished to remain anonymous) during my brief visit to the campus on orientation weekend, at least three buildings on campus are haunted. The science and technology building is haunted by a male figure who has been seen walking down the hall. Footsteps have been heard inside the locked building, and office doors have difficulties staying closed, despite being locked. The administration building is home to disembodied footsteps and voices that echo through the hall, and the bell tower seems to be a hotspot for footsteps as well. No one on campus can recall any violent acts or sudden deaths to explain the haunting. The library is also troubled by both voices and footsteps; however, the primary feature of the haunting in the library seems to be the elevator. It is prone to move between floors when empty and seems to have a mind of its own, stopping on uncalled floors or bypassing selected ones. Marie Martin, a colleague of mine on the board of PALMCOP, has told me of several incidents concerning both the elevator and the footsteps.

As mentioned above, my visit to the campus fell on orientation weekend, which meant that I could not access any of the buildings mentioned above except the administration building. However, in the hubbub of activity, any unexplained events were simply drowned out. I hope to make a return visit under quieter circumstances.

BARNWELL COUNTY

B arnwell County was formed from Orangeburg County in 1798. The county was originally known as Winton District, the borders of which ran from the Savannah River almost to the Pacific Ocean. The cession of all land belonging to the states following the ratification of the U.S. Constitution required that the lines be redrawn. The current Barnwell County is bordered by the state of Georgia and Allendale, Bamberg, Orangeburg and Aiken Counties. Barnwell County was named for the hero of the Tuscarora Indian War of 1711, Captain "Tuscarora Jack" John Barnwell. Native American activity in the area dates back before 1600 with the Yamasees serving as the major tribe in the area. During the Revolution, four skirmishes were fought in the current Barnwell County. During the Civil War, no organized skirmishes occurred, though Sherman's army passed through the county with the usual damages resulting. The Church of the Holy Apostles served as a stable for Major General Kilpatrick's cavalry mounts and the font was used as a trough. The hoof prints can still be seen on the floor of the building. Supposedly, Sherman wanted to burn Barnwell due to its resemblance in name to a leading secessionist politician from South Carolina, Robert Barnwell Rhett.

The first full-blooded African American to serve in the United States Congress, Robert Elliot, was elected to the South Carolina House from Barnwell County. No U.S. senators have come from the county, though it has supplied the state with two governors. The first of these was Johnson Hagood, a Confederate general and namesake of The Citadel's football stadium. This is an appropriate honor as Hagood was the first Citadel alumni to become governor. The second was Joseph Harley, who succeeded

Burnet Maybank as governor upon Maybank's election to the U.S. Senate in December 1941. Harley served as governor until his death in February 1942. To date, he is the last governor of South Carolina to die in office. Harley is best remembered for being part of the "Barnwell Ring" that dominated South Carolina's state government for many years. The other members included longtime Speaker of the state House of Representatives Solomon Blatt and longtime state Senator Edgar Brown. Brown is best known now as the Democratic nominee for the U.S. Senate whom Strom Thurmond defeated in 1954 via write-in ballot; the state had been solidly Democratic up until that point.

The Barnwell County Courthouse in Barnwell is home to the only extant working vertical sundial in the U.S. The county is the birthplace of soul singer and entertainer James Brown, "The Godfather of Soul"; Arthur Wayne, noted ornithologist; and one of the first Baptist missionaries to China, Louis Shook. Part of the U.S. government's Savannah River Site is located in Barnwell County. Barnwell is also home to the Possum Creep Festival.

HEALING SPRINGS:
LAND BELONGS TO THE LORD, LEGALLY

Although it is not a ghostly haunt, Healing Springs, also known as Boylston Springs, is a site too unusual not to put in a book like this. In July 1944, Lute Boylston went to the Barnwell County Courthouse and filed a rather odd deed. He deeded the acre of land surrounding the springs that bore his family name to God, making Healing (or Boylston) Springs the only property on earth legally God's property. The springs have been renowned in the area since before the Revolution when Native Americans used them to recover from injuries and illnesses. According to local lore, wounded British troops were led there by their Cherokee allies, and after a day or two of taking the waters, the men were back to full strength. Locals swear by the waters and the site is recognized as part of South Carolina's Heritage Corridor. The story of the springs and the Boylston family is best told by Raymond Boylston in his book, *Healing Springs*.

On my visit to the area, I arrived on a Sunday afternoon after a three-hour drive. Several men were dutifully filling jugs with the clear pure water from spigots placed over the sources of the springs. I decided to try some and grabbed an empty Gatorade bottle from my back seat. The atmosphere of the place was very church-like, calm and peaceful, even in the heat of a Carolina summer. I immediately got a much-needed jolt of energy and went on my way.

HILDA:
THE TRAIN DOESN'T RUN ANYMORE, DOES IT?

The story of the haunting in Hilda is one of the many I have found online that almost sound too good to be true. According to the account, steam engines and rail cars have been heard through the center of town almost every night between midnight and dawn. This occurs despite the complete absence of any tracks remaining in place in downtown Hilda. In fact, the only surviving trace of the tracks is the wide swath of grass that has grown up over the gravel rail bed and the restored century-old Seaboard Coast Line depot, now used as a venue for worship services and concerts.

Naturally, I decided to check it out as the story combined two of my great passions, trains and ghosts. No wrecks or deaths had been reported on the tracks in Hilda, so my enthusiasm dipped a bit, but I remained confident. I arrived in Hilda about 11:45 p.m. on a Friday night in August. I rolled down my car windows and parked across the former tracks and waited. I waited until about 12:30 a.m. and then headed back home. I did not hear anything unusual, but I may have quit too soon. However, the prospect of a three-hour drive home did help dim my gusto for further waiting. Hopefully, your visit will be a bit more productive than mine.

LYNDHURST, A.K.A. BOILING SPRINGS:
MORE GHOSTS THAN PEOPLE

The community of Lyndhurst, in southern Barnwell County near the Allendale County line, is apparently THE haunted hotspot of Barnwell County. The area is haunted by voices, which are described as being in happy conversation, though the topic under discussion is as unclear as the words are. The voices apparently drift up the sidewalks toward the doors of the homes in the area, but when the visitors are greeted and the doors are opened, the entries appear empty. The voices date back to the early nineteenth century and no explanation has ever been offered for the curious phenomenon.

At a home known as "Liberty Hill," a lady in black has been seen. Perhaps she is connected with the Gaunt family who lived there, but no one seems to know for sure. One source names the lady in black as a Mrs. Cater and claims that she is only seen by members of the Gaunt or "Gantt" families, but no connection has been found as yet.

According to different accounts, the old one-room schoolhouse in the area is haunted by either one or two former teachers. A male teacher whose service predates the Civil War has been seen walking around the building a bit above ground level, and a former female teacher has been seen standing in the doorway of the old school at dusk. Stories vary on the cause of her death. She either lost her sweetheart in the Civil War and died from a broken heart (or suicide), or she simply died from an illness like malaria, yellow fever or cholera. Her appearance at the school may have given rise to the legend of the Lady in Black.

Boiling Springs Presbyterian Church has been the focal point of two hauntings as well. In the first case, a "blood-curdling" scream issued from the empty church brought the men of the community out in the middle of the night with guns at the ready. Nothing was ever found, and the noise was attributed to an animal that had entered the building and was unable to immediately exit. The second story concerns the church cemetery. According to this version, the cries issued not from the building, but from the mismatched graves of two little girls who died after eating either poisoned grapes or poisonous wild berries. Once the grave markers were corrected, the cries stopped.

When I passed through the area, the serenity of the area caught my attention, but I did not hear any unearthly voices or piteous cries. I decided not to approach the old schoolhouse as it was after dark and I did not have permission to enter it. Hopefully, I can get back and do a more thorough exploration, as the site deserves in-depth study.

HAGOOD'S MILL CEMETERY: COULD BE GHOST LIGHTS, COULD BE KIDS

According to internet sources, Hagood's Mill Cemetery is the site of an unusual haunting. The cemetery is laid out in an odd circular format with the oldest burials in the center. Green, blue and yellow lights have been seen both floating through the trees and shooting up into the sky in an arc from the site. An especially strange feature of this haunting is the ghost of a skeletal dog that appears on the trail leading into the cemetery. This particular ghost brings to mind the ancient ritual of inhumation of a living thing to serve as the guardian of an important or sacred site, which was practiced by the Celts and Romans, neither of whom ever made it to inland South Carolina.

I attempted to find this cemetery but was unsuccessful because the locals were leery of sending a complete stranger to the site. I also personally feel that cemeteries are poor candidates for hauntings as few people want to hang out in such a creepy and depressing place. However, I would like to commend the locals for their attempts to protect the cemetery from potential vandals and trespassers, and I hope that on my next visit I'll be able to find the site. From the description of the lights, I feel the haunting is more than likely a combination of swamp gas, that old reliable explanation for any ghost light, and local kids with bottle rockets. I hope I can be proved wrong.

CALHOUN COUNTY

C alhoun County was formed in 1908 from parts of Orangeburg and Lexington Counties. The county was named for John C. Calhoun, the only vice-president to date from South Carolina, among his other achievements. Calhoun County is bordered by Richland, Sumter, Clarendon, Orangeburg and Lexington Counties. It is the smallest county in area in South Carolina. Native American activity in the area dates back to the Mississippian and Woodland prehistoric cultures of about 5000 BC up to the trading activities between the whites, Cherokees and Catawbas about 1750. Other tribes found in the area included the Santees and the Congarees. Calhoun County was the site of five minor Revolutionary skirmishes and one fairly well-known battle, Fort Motte. Fort Motte was a family home that was used as an ammunition depot by the British. The lady of the house, Rebecca Motte, whose husband was fighting for the American cause elsewhere, supplied General Francis Marion with fire arrows to destroy both the house and the ammunition inside. Following this rather unusual bombardment, the British commander surrendered and both sides assisted in extinguishing the fire on the house's roof. During the Civil War, no armed confrontations occurred, but Sherman's army did pass through the area after leaving Columbia a burned out shell.

No South Carolina governors or U.S. senators have come from Calhoun County yet. However, Marion Gressette, a longtime state senator from Calhoun County, helped kill the attempted ratification of the Equal Rights Amendment (ERA) by South Carolina as the chair of the State Senate Judiciary Committee. The failure of South Carolina to ratify the ERA helped to slow the momentum of the amendment, eventually killing it nationally. While Gressette began his career as a staunch foe of integration, he ended it as a champion of South Carolina State University, the major African American University in South Carolina. The best-known person with a Calhoun County tie is Julia Peterkin, who won the 1928 Pulitzer Prize for fiction for her novel *Scarlet Sister Mary*. Peterkin is buried at the county seat in Saint Matthews.

THE DEVIL LEFT HIS MARK AT FORT MOTTE

According to a legend passed down by Nell Graydon, noted South Carolina folklorist, the Devil paid a visit to the Fort Motte area before the Revolution. One stormy evening, he visited a very devout elderly couple and requested overnight shelter from the storm. As the night went on, the visitor kept steering the conversation toward religion, attempting to cause the older man to commit blasphemy or some other transgression. His wife decided that prayer would help resolve the problem and the visitor fled. Just outside the cabin, Satan left his hoof print on a large granite boulder in the yard.

Of course this tale inspired me to play "find the needle in the haystack." I took off to Fort Motte early one Saturday morning and arrived about ten a.m. The area around the present community of Fort Motte is a tranquil sea of green fields of cotton and tobacco broken occasionally by light woods and large granite boulders. I checked the boulders I could see from the road and did not have to tramp through the fields to reach. Sadly, I came to the conclusion that the hoof print has either been weathered away over the centuries or the stone has been used to decorate a local home. If you have ties to the area or other inside information, someone may lead you to it and tell you the tale far better than I could. But I tried to track it down.

OLD CALHOUN COUNTY HEALTH DEPARTMENT HAUNTED BY BARGAINS AND...

The internet is a huge help to researchers of all kinds, especially those of us interested in ghost lore and other local color. I have found many interesting accounts and have been able to prove to my own satisfaction at least several. The account of the haunting at the Old Calhoun County Health Department building in Saint Matthews is one of these intriguing tales. According to my source, the building is haunted by the apparition of a lady in a red dress in addition to faucets that cut on and off by themselves and the (seemingly ever present) disembodied footsteps and voices that ring through the empty halls and offices. The version I found online said the events occurred at anytime, so I felt confident of success as I headed out to verify it.

In August 2006, I finally got to check out the old building. It is located on a small pond in a park-like setting, which immediately concerned me as I then knew where the story had its roots. An easily accessible scenic spot offering some privacy in a small town—I knew the local teens had discovered its charms already. However, I pressed on. The building is currently being used as a thrift store by a group called Calhoun County Cares. The proceeds go to assist the elderly and others in need and provide a small pool of funds for renovations to the building. After browsing and finding a few paperbacks, I asked one of the volunteers about the haunting. She was in a hurry to get home, as it was almost closing time, but she did tell me that she had not witnessed anything extraordinary happen while she was there. She asked a colleague about anything odd happening to her and was told that the lights were prone to go on and off and the faucets acted up on occasion, but the lady felt it was just an old building and certainly not a ghost. Nothing odd occurred during my visit, and since I live too far away to volunteer with Calhoun County Cares, I'll have to recommend the site to bargain hunters rather than ghost hunters. As far as those interested in the park-like scenery, I was told that the police regularly patrol the area, so I would advise against it.

EDGEFIELD COUNTY

E dgefield County was formed in 1785 from the Old Ninety Six District, one of the twenty original counties in South Carolina. It is bordered by the state of Georgia and McCormick, Greenwood, Saluda and Aiken Counties; all the counties listed were at one time part of the original territory of Edgefield County. The source of the name of Edgefield is the fact that the county was located on both the edge of Indian territory and at the border of South Carolina and Georgia. Native American tribes with influence in the area included the Cherokees, Creeks and the Saluda. The county suffered from sporadic raids prior to 1780, and Indian traces date back to prior to 500 AD. Four Revolutionary skirmishes occurred in the modern territory of the county. Though no Civil War encounters happened in Edgefield County, Francis W. Pickens, former U.S. minister to the court of the Russian tsar under U.S. President Buchanan, was governor at the time of the attack on Fort Sumter in Charleston Harbor.

Ten South Carolina governors are claimed by Edgefield County, though several are also claimed by later counties. Six of these governors are from modern-day Edgefield County. Best known of these is "Pitchfork Ben" Benjamin Tillman who also served as U.S. senator and was the father of The South Carolina Constitution of 1895 that disenfranchised most African American voters for over fifty years. Other Edgefield governors of South Carolina included Milledge Bonham who fought in both the Mexican and Civil Wars and served in the Confederate Congress between stints as a general in the Civil War. He was governor when Sherman invaded South Carolina after his seizure of Savannah. Another governor, Andrew Pickens Jr., was the namesake of the Revolutionary partisan leader known as the "Wizard Owl" General Andrew Pickens Sr., Pierce Butler and J.C. Sheppard, who was governor during the Charleston Earthquake of 1886, also served their state as governor.

The county also claims five lieutenant governors of South Carolina, including James Tillman, the nephew of "Pitchfork Ben" and murderer of N.G. Gonzales, as well as the founding editor of *The State* newspaper in 1903. Former Confederate generals and Edgefield County natives M.C. Butler and M.W. Gary were the source of the "Edgefield Plan" which was the blueprint for the redemption of the state through fraud, intimidation and violence following Reconstruction. U.S. senators from Edgefield include the aforementioned Ben Tillman, J.C. Sheppard and M.C. Butler; Andrew P. Butler, co-author of the Kansas-Nebraska Act; and J. Strom Thurmond, who also served as governor.

Strom Thurmond was both the oldest and longest serving U.S. senator at the time of his death at age one hundred. Thurmond was also the nominee of the "Dixiecrats" in 1948, running on a strongly anti-integration ticket. He was later one of the first senators from a former Confederate state to hire an African American staffer. Thurmond won election to the U.S. Senate as a write-in candidate in 1954 after disagreeing with the selection of Edgar Brown by the State Democratic Executive Committee to replace Burnet Maybank on the ballot following Maybank's death. He became the first and so far only person ever elected to the U.S. Senate via write-in ballots, and he was also one of the first Southern politicians to switch from the Democratic to the Republican parties. Senator Thurmond also holds the current record for the longest filibuster in the U.S. Senate, twenty-four hours and eighteen minutes against the Civil Rights Act of 1957.

Other notables from Edgefield County include Confederate General James Longstreet of Gettysburg fame and U.S. Congressman Preston Brooks, who is infamous for caning U.S. Senator Charles Sumner of Massachusetts following a speech of Sumner's that indirectly insulted Senator A.P. Butler of South Carolina who was Brooks's uncle. Brooks became a hero to Southern secessionists, receiving hundreds of canes as gifts. He resigned his seat in Congress to avoid censure but was unanimously reelected. Louis Wigfall, a U.S. senator from Texas who resigned after Lincoln's election and served in the Confederate Congress, was also born in Edgefield County

The *Edgefield Advertiser* newspaper has been published under the same name since 1836 and is one of the oldest continually published newspapers in South Carolina. Noted historian Francis Simpkins, author of studies of post–Civil War politics in South Carolina and an early gender study focusing on women in the Confederacy, was born in the county. John Swearingen, the first blind graduate from the University of South Carolina and longtime state superintendent of education (1909-1922), was also born in Edgefield County.

SPEAKING OF STROM

As mentioned in the brief history of Edgefield County above, J. Strom Thurmond has left an indelible mark on the whole of modern South Carolina and especially his home county. Due to the length of his political career, he is one of the few men to hold office in post-Civil War America who received votes from Confederate veterans. He was also a decorated veteran of the Normandy invasion. However, as fascinating as he was as a person, I was curious about any possible sightings of the senator after his death. I found a brief mention in an article on South Carolina ghosts that his former law office was haunted. Reportedly, people have heard the rhythmic smacks and grunts of a man exercising and a soft voice counting in his former office. As Senator Thurmond was known to workout daily and do headstands to improve his vigor, I believe this could be him. Sadly, no one replied to a phone message left with the new occupants of the building, and the local newspaper had not heard the story. So I must say that one day I'll figure it out—I hope.

CEDAR GROVE PLANTATION:
ONE SENTENCE IN ONE SOURCE

Cedar Grove Plantation was built by John Blocker about 1790. Over its history, Cedar Grove has been owned by members of two noted South Carolina families, the Izards and the Middletons. It was placed on the National Register of Historic Places in 1971. The original external kitchen and at least one slave cabin are still standing. The house is now run as a bed-and-breakfast and features a pool, herb and flower gardens, hand-carved woodwork—especially the mantles—and hand-painted French wallpaper in the parlor.

According to the book *Country Roads of South Carolina* by Dan and Carol Thalimer, the single guest room is haunted. The other guest accommodation, a two room suite, is undisturbed. No further details are given to the brief account and attempts to contact the owners for details and clarification were unsuccessful. I would recommend a visit and wish you good luck. I feel sure the beautiful surroundings will make the possibility of not seeing a ghost easier to take.

IS THE "QUEEN OF THE CONFEDERACY" REALLY GONE?

This story more properly belongs in Aiken County as that is where the house in question currently is located, but since the possible ghost lived and died in Edgefield, I'll tell it here. Lucy Holcombe Pickens was born in 1832 in Tennessee and grew up in Texas. She was so renowned a beauty that not even the Mississippi state legislature was immune to her, as that august body recessed in her honor. Her ties to South Carolina and Edgefield County began in 1858 when she met Colonel Francis W. Pickens, a member of a noted South Carolina family with ties to the "Wizard Owl" of the Revolution, Andrew Pickens Sr. He was a former congressman who had just lost a bid for a U.S. Senate seat but was being considered for a diplomatic post. He was also twenty-seven years her senior and twice widowed, but she agreed to marry him if he took the appointment as U.S. minister to Russia. He did so and they were married in April 1858. Their only daughter, Olga Pickens, was born at the Winter Palace in Saint Petersburg, Russia, and Tsar Alexander II and the Tsarina were the child's godparents. In fact, the tsar gave Olga a lifelong nickname, "Douschka," which meant "darling" in Russian. With the turmoil in the South rising to a fever pitch with the looming election of Republican Abraham Lincoln to the Presidency, the Pickens family returned home in August 1860. The friendship between a Southern slave owner and the tsar who freed Russia's serfs is a historical fact that defies belief. As the saying goes, "there's a novel there somewhere."

After returning home, Francis Pickens was elected governor of South Carolina in December 1860, just three days before the state left the Union. He served as governor through the blockade of and the firing on Fort Sumter, which Lucy watched from a Charleston rooftop. He served until 1862. Lucy sold jewels given to her as a gift by the tsar to equip a Confederate unit, The Holcombe Legion, and was the only woman to appear on Confederate money, appearing on three issues of $100 bills and one issue of the $1 bill. She died at her home, Edgewood, in 1899 and was buried with her husband and daughter.

In 1929, Mrs. Eulalie Salley of Aiken bought Edgewood and decided to move it to Aiken, specifically to Kalmia Hill, where one of the earliest recorded appearances of the famed "Red Shirts" of the 1876 campaign to elect Wade Hampton III governor occurred. Mrs. Salley was a noted suffragist and was the first female realtor in South Carolina. Mrs. Salley was told at the time that Mrs. Pickens haunted her former home and would not take the move well. The guest room during the ownership of Mrs. Salley was formerly Lucy Pickens's bedroom. Visitors reported smelling a strong perfume and hearing the swish of silk skirts and the rustle of petticoats when the lights were turned on. Other visitors reported the feeling of not being alone in the room or of being watched. Mrs. Salley never reported any odd events. The house is on the National Register of Historic Places and is privately owned. When I called to confirm the story, I was told that the house was not haunted in the strongest terms. I have included the story due to its historical interest. Please do not disturb the current owners.

GREENWOOD COUNTY

G reenwood County was formed in 1897 from Abbeville and Edgefield Counties. It is bordered by Abbeville, Laurens, Newberry, Saluda, Edgefield and McCormick Counties. The county was either named for the plantation of John C. McGehee, who later moved to Florida and served as chair of the Florida Secession Convention, or for the green of the forests found in the area, though most historians favor the McGehee origin. Greenwood County was a center of Cherokee culture and features several mounds and other artifacts dating to before 1400 AD and was on the course of a major trading route from the Savannah River valley to Cherokee centers in North Carolina and Tennessee. Other tribes from the area include the Creeks, who staged several raids in 1764. Lander University, the state's smallest public-funded undergraduate university is located in Greenwood. Four Revolutionary War battles occurred in the county, including three at the Star Fort and British supply center at Old Ninety Six. (The Star Fort and the surrounding area will be the focus of our attention shortly.)

No Civil War battles or encounters occurred in the county, but the first Ladies Soldiers Aid Society in the Confederacy was founded at Mount Moriah Baptist Church on July 4, 1861. No U.S. senators have come from Greenwood County, but two governors have. John Gary Evans was governor and president of the State Constitutional Convention in 1895 (though Ben Tillman dominated the proceedings) and is the youngest elected governor to date in the history of the state. C.A. Smith replaced Governor Coleman Blease when Blease resigned five days before the end of his term to take a seat in the U.S. Senate. His term is the shortest of any governor in the state's history. Greenwood County was also the home of Francis Salvador, the first

Jew to serve in elective office from South Carolina and the first Jew known to have died for the cause of American independence when he was ambushed by Cherokees loyal to the British Crown in 1776. Greenwood County is also the birthplace of Benjamin Mays, former President of Morehouse College in Atlanta and mentor to Rev. Martin Luther King Jr.

A bit more of an eccentric notable from Greenwood County was Bill Voiselle, who played professional baseball for the Boston Braves, New York Giants and Chicago Cubs from 1942 to 1950. He became the first player to ever wear his hometown on his jersey when he received permission to wear number ninety-six in honor of his birthplace. Louis Wright, scholar and director of the Folger Shakespeare Library, was born in Greenwood, as was J. Fred Buzhardt Jr. who served as President Richard Nixon's attorney during the Watergate Scandal. Buzhardt also revealed the existence of the eighteen-and-a-half minute gap on one of the key Oval Office tapes. In 1870, Allen University was begun as Payne Institute in Greenwood County. The school relocated to Columbia in 1880. Greenwood is home to Park Seed Company and hosts the South Carolina Festival of Flowers every year.

Brewer Middle School

Brewer Middle School was founded as Brewer Normal Institute by the Congregational Church after the Civil War to educate newly freed slaves. It was the first school for African Americans in Greenwood County. Brewer Normal Institute served the African American community until after integration, when the current name was given to the building. According to an online source, the school's proud history was marred at some point when a cheerleader was killed by a football player following a game. The report supplies no motive, no result for the game, not even a method of murder; though I suppose one is meant to use their imagination, I'm sure. She was supposedly killed under the stage in the gymnasium and haunts the areas near the stage and the furnace room. No one I spoke to at the modern Brewer Middle School had heard the stories before. In fact, the school secretary asked me if I meant the original building, meaning Brewer Normal and seemed to be upset at the slander I was attempting to place on the school.

Investigating rumors of a haunting in a school setting is especially difficult under the best of circumstances, which would include knowing an employee on site, having a good rapport with the administration and respecting the hard work of the faculty and students. After Columbine and the other unfortunate incidents over the last few years, schools are naturally leery of allowing strangers to roam the halls at odd times and especially if they are looking for ghosts. So, the job of the researcher is made even more difficult. Very few schools seem to be eager to embrace any ghostly legends found in their halls, as the lady above has shown, so all I could do with the report at Brewer Middle School was call the school and attempt to get the tale verified. It's not as much fun as seeing a ghost in the flesh, but even us ghost storytellers have to obey state and federal laws.

WARE SHOALS HIGH SCHOOL

According to local lore and online accounts, the ghost of the first superintendent (though I think principal is more likely) of Ware Shoals High School roams the auditorium balcony and appears in the gymnasium. I found it to be strange that this gentleman and scholar is unnamed in either version of the tale. Another odd event at the school is the claim that if you drive around the front of the school (I assume at night though this is not specified), a light will suddenly glow.

This account was one of the more frustrating to research in this book. The school denied that anything unusual occurred on the property and that all lights in the front of the building were accounted for. The lack of information about the man's identity made the chore of nailing down any details or a timeframe for the start of the legend problematic at best. Sadly, I have to write off the legend of the haunting at Ware Shoals High School as a tale told by seniors to frighten and cow underclassmen and as an excuse for the occasional practical joke.

THE STAR FORT AT NINETY SIX: HAUNTED HISTORY

The Star Fort at Ninety Six is one of the most historically significant sites in South Carolina. Ninety Six was named from the mistaken belief that it was located ninety-six miles from the major Cherokee town at Keowee. As the modern town's zip code is 29666, it is jocularly known as the town with a number for a name and its name in its zip code. Three different Revolutionary War battles occurred at the site. Among its other notable facts, it was the site of the first major land battle of the Revolution in the Southern Colonies, the strongest fortification in the South, the site of the longest siege undertaken by the Continental army and the last British outpost to be held by them in inland South Carolina.

The final siege at Ninety Six was led by Major General Nathaniel Greene who arrived at the fort with 1,000 men in May 1781 and decided a siege was the only way to take the heavily fortified outpost. The garrison inside was commanded by Lieutenant Colonel John Cruger who led a force of 550 American Tories and about 100 local Loyalist families, one British regular and some slaves lured by British promises of emancipation if the British regained control over their colonies. Cruger himself was an American, son of a leading New York Tory family. Colonel Thaddeus Kosciusko, a Polish professional solider and the only person on the American side with any true military training, served as Greene's chief engineer. He recommended focusing on reducing the Star Fort at the eastern end of the compound, as it was the strongest point.

The Patriots hurt their chances for quick success by digging trenches about two hundred feet from the walls and setting their artillery about four hundred feet away. Two days after Greene's arrival, the garrison opened fire on the trench diggers. Following a few volleys from the walls, about thirty Tories bayoneted the stragglers while a group of slaves stole the Patriots' entrenching tools. The Americans fell back and built a tower to fire over the walls, to which Cruger responded by sandbagging the walls and returning fire. Following an attempt to get Cruger to surrender, which was rebuffed, Greene ordered his troops to fire flaming arrows into the compound, which prompted Cruger to tear off the wooden shingles from the roofs, rendering the idea useless.

Despite Cruger's ingenuity, the defenders were struggling. Fresh rations had been used up, the salted rations were insufficient and the heat and humidity of a Carolina summer was wearing on the garrison. The only source of water was a small creek running outside the walls. A small fort was built near the creek and a covered trench connected the two stockades. Despite these precautions, the attempt to dig a well inside the main fort was a failure. In June 1781, fresh from seizing Augusta, Georgia, Lieutenant Colonel Henry "Light-Horse Harry" Lee arrived and was ordered to take the smaller creek side fort. The closeness of his trenches to the walls forced the Tory troops stationed there to send nude slaves out under cover of darkness to get water. By mid-June, Lord Rawdon, British commander in the Carolinas, was en route to relieve the thirsty garrison with two thousand British regulars. This action forced Greene to abandon the siege and try a direct assault. Following a heavy artillery barrage, the Patriots made their way over the twelve-foot-deep defensive trench in front of the walls by building a crude bridge of brush. Men with long hooked poles were ordered to remove the sandbags so the snipes in the tower could pick defenders with ease. All was going well until the defenders sent two parties of thirty men each from the rear of the stockade and hit the attackers on both flanks. After a brief hand-to-hand battle, the attackers fell back to their trenches. With Rawdon's army less than fifty miles away, Greene had to leave the field. A few weeks later, the defenders were ordered to Charleston and the Patriots seized the abandoned stronghold.

The site is now a National Historic Site under the care of the National Park Service and the usual restrictions apply, especially concerning any artifacts found on the property. The trenches and the wooden stockade are modern reconstructions but the outline of the earthen walls of the Star Fort is original. Prior to the site coming under the care of the National Park Service, bullets, buttons and other artifacts were found on the surface. Most are now displayed in the small museum on-site. The site is even more intriguing based on stories gathered over the years. Near the creek, dogs react to invisible stimuli, and harsh voices have been heard barking orders to columns of men on the march, though no one is ever seen nor have footprints been found, even after heavy rains. Reenactors of the battle camped near the old dry well inside the compound have heard voices as well.

Prior to the construction of the fort, an Indian trader named Goudy lived in the area and built a small trading post. One of the two small family cemeteries in the park is the resting place of members of this family. People have heard the sounds of children running, playing and laughing in both cemeteries, despite the complete lack of living children there. Of the one hundred soldiers who died on both sides during the siege, very few have been reburied in actual cemeteries. They probably still lie where they fell, which helps to explain the occasional return.

My only visit to the Star Fort at Ninety Six came my sophomore year at Spartanburg Methodist College when the History Club went on a field trip to tour the area. After about a thirty-minute guided tour, we were allowed to roam the park at will. The day was clear, but it was about 5:00 p.m. and beginning to get dark. A friend of mine and I wandered over by the creek hoping to find some arrowheads or other artifacts to donate to the park. Instead, we both heard the sounds of a party of men walking up the bank, with a harsh male voice saying, "We'll camp here tonight." My friend and I exchanged a quick glance and headed back to the bus leaving for Spartanburg with a bit more speed than the others. To my knowledge, activity is still ongoing, and I definitely recommend a visit, both for Revolutionary War buffs and ghost hunters alike.

HAMPTON COUNTY

Hampton County was formed in 1878 from Beaufort County. It was named for the sitting governor of South Carolina, Wade Hampton III, who laid the cornerstone for the courthouse during a visit on his reelection campaign trip through the area. Parts of the county were later lost to Allendale and Jasper Counties. Hampton County is bordered by Allendale, Bamberg, Colleton, Beaufort and Jasper Counties and by the state of Georgia. A Native American presence in the area dates back to at least 1400 AD and was first recorded by Europeans in 1539 when Hernando de Soto encountered the Yamasee tribe. Three skirmishes occurred in the county during the Revolution. The small community of McPhersonville was the site of the 1853 wedding of Theodore Roosevelt Sr. and Martha Bulloch (sometimes spelled Bullock) at Stoney Creek Presbyterian Church. The happy couple is best known as the parents of U.S. President Theodore Roosevelt and as the grandparents of First Lady Eleanor Roosevelt (Mrs. Franklin Delano Roosevelt). During the Civil War, McPhersonville was burned by Sherman's troops. The county was the site of a skirmish at Lawtonville as well as one of the first major battles waged by Sherman's army after the fall of Atlanta at Broxton Bridge. The latter skirmish was part of the flanking maneuvers involved in the crossing of the Salkehatchie River mentioned under Rivers Bridge in Bamberg County.

No U.S. senators have called Hampton County home, but the county has given South Carolina one governor, Miles McSweeney, who completed the term of W.H. Ellerbe upon his death and then won a term of his own. Clara McMillan, the widow of Congressman Thomas McMillan, won a special election to fill the seat of her late husband and served from 1939 to 1941.

She was the first woman to win election to Congress from South Carolina, though Elizabeth (Liz) Patterson later became the first to win a regular election to Congress from South Carolina. Two other notable natives of Hampton County were James and Julius Fields, African American brothers who became noted dancers and choreographers in Hollywood after 1950. Following the murder of Reverend Martin Luther King Jr. on April 4, 1968, violence broke out in the town of Hampton and some 120 other cities throughout the country. Hampton is also host to the Watermelon Festival, which began in 1939 and is the oldest continuous festival in South Carolina.

OAK GROVE PLANTATION

Despite the long history of settlement in the Hampton County area, I have managed to find very few stories to tell about the ghosts in the area. According to an owner of the house, the old Augusta Stage Coach Inn, better known in the area as Oak Grove Plantation or the Richardson place, is haunted. Several orbs have been reported in photographs taken in different rooms at different times. The orbs were all caught in motion and were of different sizes. None of the orbs were visible to the naked eye. To me, this implies actual ghostly activity more than the classic shots of static or yellowish globs of light. I feel that motion and a variety in sizes and colors signify at least remedial intelligence, whereas the motionless images imply merely a release of long built-up dust. The house was used by General Sherman as his headquarters during his well-known trip through the area in 1865 and is mentioned in his memoirs. This use of the house not only explains how the property escaped the torches of the bummers but may also explain one feature of the reported haunting. Even though the main house burned in 2000 and has since been renovated, local lore still mentions sightings of Union soldiers staring out of windows, apparently still on guard duty, even when the house has been vacant. Other odd reports over the years include heavy footsteps on the main staircase, men's voices in quiet though indistinct conversation and the various bangs, creaks and bumps associated with old houses, even those that are not haunted. The current owners of the house claim not to have seen or heard anything out of the ordinary and remind potential visitors that the property is posted no hunting or trespassing and that it is private property; please respect their wishes. I have included the story simply due to the historic nature of the haunting.

LEXINGTON COUNTY

L exington County was formed in 1804 from part of the territory of the original Orangeburg District. It is bounded by Newberry, Richland, Calhoun, Orangeburg, Aiken and Saluda Counties. The county was named for Lexington, Massachusetts, site of the first battle of the Revolution. Lexington County later lost parts of its area to Aiken and Calhoun Counties upon their establishment. Native American activity in the area dates from 1000 BC, and the Woodland, Deptford and Mississippian cultures were present prior to the first century AD. The Cherokee, Creek and Catawba tribes are the major source of more modern remains. The Catawba traded in the area, especially at Fort Granby across the Congaree River from modern Columbia, while the Cherokee raided the area during the Cherokee War of 1760–61. During the Revolution, Fort Granby was the site of two of the seven armed encounters that occurred in the county, and during the Civil War, Lexington County was the site of Sherman's initial bombardment of Columbia prior to occupying the city in 1865.

Only one U.S. senator and governor was born in Lexington County, John Taylor, who held both offices, though South Carolina Governor George B. Timmerman Jr. lived in the county briefly. Floyd Spence, the first Republican since Reconstruction to serve in both the South Carolina and United States House of Representatives, as well as the South Carolina Senate, lived in the county and is buried there. Juanita Hipps—who served in the Army Nurse Corps during World War II as a Lieutenant Colonel and wrote a memoir, *I Served on Bataan*, which was turned into an Oscar-nominated film titled *So Proudly We Hail*—was born in Swansea. The county is also the site of the former Columbia Army Air

Force Base, which served as a training site for Lieutenant Colonel James Doolittle's Raiders before the successful bombing raid on Tokyo, Japan, on April 18, 1942.

Celebrities from Lexington County include talk show host Leeza Gibbons and Revolutionary War heroine Emily Geiger. Geiger was carrying a message from General Greene to General Sumter and ate the paper the message was on prior to being searched so that she would not be detained as a spy. Festivals in Lexington County include the South Carolina Poultry Festival in Batesburg-Leesville, the South Carolina Peanut Festival in Pelion, the Okra Strut in Irmo and the Conagree Festival in Cayce and West Columbia. Lexington County is also the location of Lake Murray, a major recreational center in the Midlands. The community of Batesburg-Leesville was once home to (the now defunct) Leesville College, which fielded the first women's basketball team in South Carolina.

AIRPORT HIGH SCHOOL: FINALLY, A SCHOOL PROUD TO BE HAUNTED

Airport High School in Cayce, near the Columbia Metropolitan Airport, is not what most people picture when a haunted school is mentioned. The remodeled exterior and interior shout twenty-first century and the faculty and students are certainly creatures of the modern age. The school has a long and proud tradition of both academic and athletic excellence. The creation of Airport High School can in large part be credited to one man, the school's first principal, George Pair. Mr. Pair fought to have the school built and served as its first principal from 1958 to 1962. George Pair is also the reason for the haunting at the school.

George Pair loved Airport High and took great pains to ensure it would be a jewel in the crown of the educational system in Lexington County. He arrived at work early and was often the last to leave, working over many weekends to make sure things were up to his high standards. Sadly, this devotion may have helped cause his death. According to numerous accounts, Mr. Pair's favorite spot to watch over things during class changes was on the school's three hundred hall. Apparently, late one Friday evening, Mr. Pair was working in this area when he was stricken with a serious heart attack. His body was not found until the following Monday. Since then, students, teachers and staff have reported seeing a tall, well-dressed man standing on the three hundred hall with his arms crossed or with his hands on his hips watching over class changes. When I called to confirm the events, a school secretary, who is also an Airport alumna, said that Mr. Pair has been seen many, many times at different times of the day and as recently as a few years ago. She did mention that the school would prefer visitors not come simply to see the ghost, and they should obey all applicable laws while on campus, which I took as a strong hint that ghost hunters and thrill seekers were not welcome guests.

When I was in high school, several of us decided to visit Airport High to see if there was any truth to the rumors of a haunting. We arrived about 6:00 p.m. and decided to just walk around outside, as none of us wanted to try breaking and entering. We were on the back side of the building when we passed a window and saw a tall, middle-aged man standing in the center of the hall. One of my friends decided to be a smart aleck and tapped on the glass. The man turned and the fact that lockers were visible behind him, actually through him, left us convinced. We scurried back to our waiting car and immediately headed back to Lyman. No one said anything the entire ninety-minute ride, which was remarkable for that particular group, especially me. The next morning, we asked if everyone had seen the same thing and then swore to never bring it up again. Of course, I tell the story every chance I get now, some fifteen years later.

BUSBEE MIDDLE SCHOOL AND LEXINGTON HIGH SCHOOL

As I have mentioned before, most schools are not thrilled to admit to being haunted for fairly obvious reasons. However, in the interest of fully covering the subject at hand, here are two accounts from schools in Lexington County that have been denied by the administration of both the schools and the school districts, but which still flourish online. The first tale concerns Busbee Middle School, which is now Cyril B. Busbee Creative Arts Academy in Cayce. According to online sources, the "E-pod" is haunted by the ghost of a girl who fell down the stairs and broke her neck due to the lack of light. Accordingly, she wishes no one else to fall victim to this and makes sure that the light over that staircase is always on, even when school is not in session. Sadly, the school was renovated in 2004 and the person I spoke to said that the problem arose from faulty wiring and that no one had ever died on campus. I have to write this legend off as a tale told by upperclassmen to scare their younger counterparts.

The other haunting that has been denied by school authorities is at Lexington High School. According to the legend, a girl choked to death in the girl's locker room. No mention is made of whether this was an accident or murder. Since her demise, the locker and shower stall doors bang open and closed at odd intervals. The school district has issued a statement denying that any student has ever died on campus, and they denied the haunting via telephone. This story too must go in the category of stories told by seniors to spook underclassmen.

LEGENDS OF LEESVILLE (AND BATESBURG, TOO)

Batesburg-Leesville was formed by the merger of the two communities in 1994. Since the towns have merged, it is fitting that we cover the ghost stories of each in one section. The Bond-Bates-Hartley House was built in 1795 by John P. Bond and was later home to the Bates family, for which the community of Batesburg was named. It was added to the National Register of Historic Places in 1982. Local lore reports that Mr. Bond has been seen in the house wearing a suit of antebellum vintage, and a lady in a red dress has waved to passersby from the attic window, even when the house was vacant. A piano has been known to play of its own accord as well. There is a small family graveyard across U.S. Highway 1 from the house, and a boy buried there, according to local assumption, has been seen in the garden of the Bond home and walking alongside U.S. 1. No one has identified the young man and how he is known to be a ghost is unclear, though I assume suddenly disappearing while in plain sight or appearing to be transparent would play a role.

The haunting in Leesville is a bit less cut and dried. According to an online source, a tree in downtown Leesville that was once used to hang recalcitrant slaves is haunted. The fact that a ritual is involved to call the ghost up left me a bit skeptical. The procedure is to drive around the tree three times without any headlights—I assume this should be done after dark—and then park and cut on your headlights. A male figure should then appear suspended from one of the branches.

Notwithstanding the hazards of driving around at night with no lights, especially near what I assumed to be a rather large and ancient tree, I decided to attempt to verify this legend. Upon arriving in Leesville, I asked a few folks for directions to the hanging tree. No one knew what I was talking about, which is never good. Driving through downtown, I saw no likely candidates for the dubious honor of serving as a makeshift gallows. If you decide to attempt to track this legend to its lair, be careful; the ritual described sounds more likely to make you a ghost than to summon one.

HAUNTED HOUSE IN GILBERT

Since the publication of my first book—*Ghosts of the South Carolina Upcountry*, published in 2005 by The History Press—I have done numerous book signings and storytelling appearances all over the state of South Carolina. Without fail, at least one person mentions a ghost story of their own. Most of these they will not let me use, either because they still live at the site or don't want it getting out. However, while working on this book, I went to a signing at Dutch Square Mall in Columbia. A gentleman bought a book and told me the following story. All he asked was that I not give the exact location of the house or use his name, so here goes.

The house is located in the community of Gilbert off U.S. Highway 1 and was the boyhood home of the gentleman mentioned above. The haunting, as described to me, mostly consists of auditory events. Footsteps have been heard in every room. Low voices have been heard in earnest, if indistinct, conversation that fades out when the room is entered. In one instance, a visiting family member heard a heartbeat or other rhythmic noise issuing from one of the bedrooms. She immediately cut on all the lights and blasted the television at high volume until more people arrived. Locked doors have also been seen to open and close and doorknobs have been torn from people's hands. On another occasion, a storage room door for which the man's father had lost the key and had propped open was found to be locked. Naturally, the father was very displeased in the manner of most Southern fathers of a certain generation, which meant a good whipping for the son, who denied responsibility. The next morning the door was open and unlocked and the key was still missing. The teller of this tale mentioned that the old Charleston stagecoach road once ran near the house and that Native American artifacts had been found on the property. The exact connection remains unmade, but the demeanor of the man as he told the tale left me convinced of its truth. If he suckered me, then you are his next victim, but I doubt it.

FROM SOUTH CAROLINA TO SOUTH TEXAS...FIRST TRIP

South of the community of Dixiana, between U.S. Highway 21/176/321 and Interstate 26 runs a set of CSX railroad tracks. At the intersection of railway and highway, according to both local lore and online accounts, a horrible tragedy still echoes through the years. Sometime in the 1970s, a school bus stalled on the tracks during a storm and was hit by a train. According to the account, if you put your car in neutral and park in the center of the tracks on a rainy day, your car will be pushed over the tracks. If, like me, your car goes a while between washes, you may see small handprints appear after you have been pushed clear of the tracks.

Sadly, I could find no mention in the local papers of this awful event, and I was immediately struck by the similarities between this and another tragic school bus and train meeting that occurred at a crossing located south of San Antonio on Villa Main Road. According to this version, the accident occurred in the early 1940s on a cold and misty afternoon. The poor visibility, lack of crossing guards and noise on the bus prevented the driver from seeing the oncoming freight. Everyone on the bus was killed instantly. When the area was developed, the subdivision that grew up around the crossing had streets that were named after the young victims of the wreck. The events surrounding the South Carolina accident are similar to the events recounted above, with the added detail that the approach to the crossing has a slight uphill grade. Drivers who have suddenly applied the brakes at the crossing in Texas have reported having rear windshields shattered by the force of the children pushing on their cars, and some drivers have been known to coat their cars with flour to make the handprints easier to see. People living near the intersection have also reported hearing moaning on some late afternoons.

I have not been to San Antonio to investigate the Villa Main Road crossing, but I have checked out the one near Dixiana. While I did not see any child-sized handprints on my dirty car, I did seemingly coast uphill and over the tracks while in neutral. Sadly, I was not brave enough to slam on the brakes and see what would happen to my rear windshield, though it was more out of concern for the cost of replacing the windshield than out of worry about ghosts. If you have confidence in your insurance policy and company, feel free to try it yourself.

MCCORMICK COUNTY

McCormick County was formed from parts of Abbeville, Edgefield and Greenwood Counties in 1916. It was named for inventor Cyrus McCormick, inventor of the mechanical reaper, who was a major landowner in the area. The county is bounded by the State of Georgia and Abbeville, Greenwood and Edgefield Counties. Native American activity in the area dates from about 1000 AD and was focused on the Cherokee, Creek and other tribes. The Cherokee staged several raids during the Cherokee War of 1760–61, and the Creeks staged some raids prior to relocating further to the southwest in 1764. Several Indian mounds of uncertain origin are located in the county. McCormick County was the site of Fort Charlotte, whose seizure by state militia under Major James Mayson on July 12, 1775, was the first overt act of war in South Carolina. McCormick County was also the site of two other skirmishes during the Revolution. No known armed encounters occurred during the Civil War.

Only one governor of South Carolina has resided in what is now McCormick County, George McDuffie, who later served as a U.S. senator. He was also the father-in-law of Wade Hampton III, Civil War hero, Redeemer governor and U.S. Senator. In fact, the county is best known as the site of Reverend Moses Waddell's Willington Academy, located in the community of Willington. Reverend Waddell was a major early educational mentor and trained both John C. Calhoun and Unionist leader James L. Petigru, Calhoun's major opponent in antebellum South Carolina politics. Unusual sites on the National Register of Historic Places include the Dorn Gold Mine, one of the last active gold mines in the state, and Bradley's (or

Long Cane) Covered Bridge, one of the last remaining covered bridges still intact in South Carolina in its original location.

BADWELL CEMETERY: HISTORY, "HANTS" AND A TROLL

Badwell Cemetery was the family burial grounds of first the Gibert family and later the Petigru family. Reverend Jean (or John) Louis Gibert was the leader of the French Huguenot settlement at New Bordeaux, which was established about 1764 in order to allow the Huguenots the freedom to worship as they saw fit and to escape the growing persecution of French Protestantism following the revocation of the Edict of Nantes. Currently, only one house remains from New Bordeaux, the Guillebeau House, which was built about 1770. Some of the settlers planted vines and produced the first commercial wine made in South Carolina.

James Petigru was the dominant anti-nullification and Unionist leader in South Carolina. His strong opposition to positions favored by the states rights faction led by John C. Calhoun limited his office holding to one term in the South Carolina House of Representatives from 1831 to 1832. Prior to that, he served as state attorney general for a term before he split with Calhoun. Petigru may not have held a U.S. Senate seat or served as governor, but his role as a Unionist leader served to influence postwar leaders like Benjamin Perry and James Orr. James Petigru was also the grandson of Reverend Jean Louis Gibert.

To my knowledge, neither of these distinguished gentlemen are features in the haunting at Badwell Cemetery. The account I found online claims that a troll has been seen walking the perimeter just outside the stone wall! The gate (no longer on site) was iron and featured a life-size grim reaper. Many odd events have occurred, though the website does not give any details; however, I will mention one that occurred on my only visit.

I visited Badwell Cemetery on a whim after finding the account of the haunting online. The site has a state historical highway marker nearby, so it's easy to find, though only visit if you will treat the area with the respect the cemetery deserves. I arrived about 8:00 p.m. on a Saturday evening a few summers ago. After walking through the cemetery and transcribing a few of the stones, I was heading back to my car when I glanced back to make sure I had everything and saw three white lights flit through the trees just above eye level. Now, I'm six feet (and some change) tall, so these lights were too high and large to be fireflies flying in formation. They passed through a gravestone and vanished—did not flicker out, did not break, just simply vanished as suddenly as they came. I nodded, kept walking to my car and continued home. Some things just defy explanation.

THE OLD MILL

This story is included merely to demonstrate the frustration that can spring from working on a book like this. On a website devoted to reader submitted ghost stories, I found the following entry for the town of McCormick. The tale claimed that if you took a stroll past the mill at night and peeked in the windows, you would see the faces of those workers that had died on the job and would later feel like you were being followed by some invisible being or force. My, what a creepy tale, right? Sadly, no one at the McCormick County Library had even heard of the mill being haunted, there are no records of the mill being any less safe than dozens of others in the region and I could not find any front-page articles about disasters at the site. So, despite my best efforts, I could not confirm the tale. In fact, on my visit to McCormick, I tried to peek in the windows of the mill, but the barbed wire atop the chain link fence stopped me a good fifty feet from the building.

THE MURDER OF PEGGY DONALD:
A GRUESOME SENTENCE FOR A GRUESOME CRIME

On occasion, while researching local histories for legends and lore of bygone days, I happen to stumble across some rather disturbing tales. However, the story of the murder of Peggy Donald and the fitting punishment meted out to her killer even gave me pause. Mrs. Donald was home in April 1830 awaiting the return of her husband, West Donald, from a (hopefully) successful trading trip into Cherokee territory in Georgia. A field slave named Jerry, leased by Mr. Donald from his owner, a Ms. McQuerns, rushed into the house and sexually assaulted Mrs. Donald while she was preparing a meal. When Mrs. Donald attempted to escape by leaping over the rail fence in the yard, Jerry cut off her hands with a meat axe before she could vault the fence. Jerry then stuffed the still alive but in shock Mrs. Donald into the blazing fireplace in the kitchen. Thankfully, Mr. Donald arrived home in time to spare his bride the flames, but she died of her injuries shortly afterward. Jerry was arrested and tried for rape with intent to murder. He was found guilty and sentenced to be burnt to death in one of Mr. Donald's fallow fields. The minister at Long Cane Associate Reformed Presbyterian Church preached Jerry's funeral sermon while the pyre was being constructed. At the end of the sermon, the pastor, Dr. John Presley, prayed with Jerry, who continued to pray until the flames killed him. This was the last execution by fire in South Carolina and the only one I have found any record of.

A person could be excused for thinking that Jerry might return to torture those who submitted him to such a fate, but they would be wrong. For according to local lore and the testimony of an anonymous Methodist minister, who happened to pick the wrong tree for a tree stand, Mrs. Donald reappears in the same field that her attacker met his end in and seems to be in the process of cooking and setting a table. Her appearance is that of an older lady with white hair wearing a shawl, and as suddenly as she appears, she vanishes. Using the directions in the source of the tale, I drove to the site hoping to get lucky and see this apparition for myself. Sadly, I struck out. It seems that Mrs. Donald only appears sporadically at best. Hopefully, on my next trip to the area, I'll have better luck.

ORANGEBURG COUNTY

The first territory to bear the name of Orangeburg District was formed in 1769 and named in honor of Prince William IV of Orange, son-in-law of King George II. Between 1785 and 1791, the district was divided into four counties: Lexington, Lewisburg, Winton and Orange. Orangeburg District was re-formed (with the exception of Barnwell District, formerly Winton) in 1798 by the merger of the remaining three districts. Over time, Orangeburg County lost territory to Lexington, Calhoun and Aiken Counties as well. Currently, Orangeburg County is bounded by Aiken, Lexington, Calhoun, Clarendon, Berkeley, Dorchester, Bamberg and Barnwell Counties. The Native American presence in the area dates from 1000 AD and the major tribes in the area were the Yamasee and the Catawba. The area suffered gravely in the Yamasee War of 1715–16, which resulted in the Yamasee leaving the area. The county was the site of the Battle of Eutaw Springs, the last major land engagement of the Revolution on August 8, 1781, and eight other skirmishes. Sherman's army passed through the county after burning Columbia in February 1865. The only governor of South Carolina from the county was R.J. Williams. Orangeburg County has yet to give the state a U.S. senator, but the county was home to Congressman Lawrence Keitt. Keitt was censured for escorting Congressman Preston Brooks to the U.S. Senate chamber when Brooks attacked Senator Sumner of Massachusetts with a cane, and he later resigned from Congress. Like Brooks, Keitt was reelected to Congress and later served the Confederacy as a congressman and as a brigadier general. He was fatally wounded at the Battle of Cold Harbor in 1864.

Orangeburg County is the location of Edisto Memorial Gardens, South Carolina State University and Claflin University—the oldest historically black institution of higher learning in South Carolina, founded in 1869. (We'll be returning to Claflin shortly.) A couple of prominent South Carolinians attended these institutions. Conservative columnist Armstrong Williams attended South Carolina State University and served as student body president, and Ernest Finney Jr., the first African American to serve as a circuit court judge in South Carolina and the first African American to serve as chief justice of the South Carolina Supreme Court, was a graduate of Claflin University and the law school at South Carolina State University. He has also served as president of South Carolina State University following his retirement from the bench.

Orangeburg County was also home to portraitist Jeremiah Theus and the birthplace of noted South Carolina historian and state archivist Alexander S. Salley. Noted entertainer Eartha Kitt was born in the community of North. Orangeburg County is also home to a couple of South Carolina festivals. Edisto Memorial Gardens hosts the Orangeburg Festival of Roses every year, and the town of Branchville, home to the first railroad junction in the world in 1830, hosts the annual "Raylrode Daze Festivul."

On February 8, 1968, Orangeburg was the site of the Orangeburg Massacre, which resulted from an anti-segregation protest at a bowling alley near the South Carolina State campus. Of the two hundred protesters present, three men were shot by police and twenty-seven were injured. The only person convicted of any crime was Cleveland Sellers, the leader of the protest and head of the local Student Nonviolent Coordinating Committee (SNCC) for supposedly inciting the riot that preceded the shootings, though he has since been pardoned for this unjust conviction. This was the first "Kent State–Style" shooting on an American university campus, though it did not receive the press coverage of the later incident. Following the murder of Reverend Martin Luther King Jr. on April 4, 1968, additional minor violence broke out in Orangeburg and some 120 other cities throughout the country.

CLAFLIN UNIVERSITY: STRAIGHT FROM THE TOP

Claflin University was founded in 1869 by the Methodist Church to assist newly freed slaves in exercising their rights as citizens. It was named for then governor of Massachusetts, William Claflin, who provided funds for the initial organization of the school. The school's charter directly prohibits discrimination of any kind among faculty, staff and students, making Claflin the first South Carolina university open to all students regardless of race, class or gender. The original Fisk Building on the university campus was designed by Robert Bates who is recognized as the first certified black architect in the United States. The building was later destroyed by fire, which is an unfortunate trend on Claflin's campus. The Reverend Dr. Lewis M. Dunton was a key figure in the success of Claflin University. He recruited former South Carolina Supreme Court Justice J.J. Wright to set up the legal program and to assist graduates in becoming members of the South Carolina Bar. Justice Wright was the only African American to serve on the South Carolina Supreme Court during Reconstruction.

Dr. Henry Tisdale, the current President of Claflin University, has made academic achievement and improving the learning environment on campus his main priorities. Examples of his efforts, aided by committed faculty members and dedicated student, include the establishment of the Claflin Honors College and the Center for Excellence in Science and Mathematics, as well as the procurement of national accreditation for more than a dozen academic programs. Graduate programs established include the Master of Business Administration, the Master of Science in Biotechnology and the Master of Education. Facilities enhancements include construction of the Living and Learning Center, Legacy Plaza, the Student Residential Center, the Music Center and the new University Chapel. Dr. Tisdale is important to this book in that he was my primary source of information on the hauntings on campus.

I met President Tisdale when I visited the campus in hopes of finding a ghost story for this chapter, as my online and print sources offered little help. I thought I would ask some students if any unusual events had occurred, and if they offered no help, I would ask campus security and staff at the library. I happened to arrive in mid-August during orientation. I thought the gentleman I saw assisting an older man was a faculty member pressed into service, but it was the president himself. I explained why I was on campus and he was very forthcoming. He explained that he had heard voices and footsteps in Tingley Memorial Hall, the main administration building (and on the National Register of Historic Places), while working alone in the building at night, but he could offer no explanation for the events. He also mentioned that Dunton Memorial Hall, the oldest girl's dormitory on campus, was haunted by former President Lewis Dunton's wife who walked the halls checking on the heirs to her former charges, as she served as house mother to the dorm during her husband's presidency. He mentioned that the original building had burned in 1955 and that Mrs. Dunton only became active after its reconstruction in 1957. Sadly, he declined my request to investigate, as it is a female-only dorm and parents might be upset by a lone male wandering the halls, even in the daytime. I thanked him for his time on such a hectic day—after all he had ignored at least two requests from other staff members over his radio and had spent about thirty minutes with me—and I continued on my way, thankful for the assistance.

RICHLAND COUNTY

Richland County was established in 1785 and is bordered by Kershaw, Fairfield, Lexington, Calhoun and Sumter Counties. The county was named by early settlers in reference to the "rich land" found along the many rivers in the area. The Native American presence in the county dates back to the start of the Common Era, with the main tribes being the Cherokees, Catawbas, Congarees and Waterees. The area mainly served as a neutral hunting ground, though during the 1760–61 Cherokee War John Pearson built a private fort in the northern part of the county; however, there is no record of any hostile activity in the area due to a fairly small population. Prior to the Revolution, several major trading paths passed through the county. Although no Revolutionary War battles occurred in the county, President George Washington did spent several nights in the area during his Southern tour in 1791. Also in 1791, Richland County lost territory to Kershaw County upon its establishment.

In 1786, the capital of South Carolina was relocated from Charleston to Columbia, the first planned city in South Carolina and the second in the United States, following Savannah, Georgia. As the site of the capital of South Carolina, Richland County was an epicenter of both the nullification and secession crises. On December 17, 1860, the First Baptist Church in Columbia was the site of the first meeting of the Secession Convention held following Lincoln's election in 1860, though a rumored smallpox outbreak led to an adjournment and reassembly in Charleston. Some scholars believe that the outbreak rumors were the product of the fears of Secessionist leaders that Columbia's atmosphere would be too moderate to declare for immediate action. For most of the Civil War, Columbia served as a manufacturing and political center for the Confederacy, though a prisoner of war camp, Camp Sorghum, was located outside the city. However, the fall of Savannah in December 1864 opened up South Carolina to Sherman's advancing troops. As the "Cradle of Secession," the state feared what retribution Sherman would exact, but most (including both civil and military authorities) felt Charleston would be hardest hit. After feints toward both Charleston and Aiken, Sherman's army headed north toward Columbia. The city surrendered on February 16, 1865, after Union troops shelled the then under construction state house, leaving scars that are now marked by six bronze stars on the marble walls of the reconstructed state house. Sadly for the student of antebellum architecture, on February 17, 1865, Columbia was in flames.

The debate over who was responsible for the blaze has persisted since the last ember was doused. Some scholars placed the blame on Confederate Commander Wade Hampton III and claimed he ordered cotton stored in the city set alight to keep it out of Union hands. Strong winds and dry weather did the rest. As Hampton was a Columbia native and later served as governor and U.S. senator from South Carolina, I doubt his culpability for the inferno. The more commonly held theory is that some of Sherman's troops, after being discovered in the act of looting, set the blaze to cover their tracks and the wind and weather then caused the flames to burn out of control. Although most scholars blame "the Yankees" for the fire, the most popular rationale is that it was set in revenge for the leading role played by the state in the sectional crises of the previous half century or so. The fact that some of Sherman's men inquired about the location of the First Baptist Church before the fire lends some credence to this view. Over one third of the city's buildings were lost including most of the government offices and the business district. Other Confederate generals with Richland County ties include Maxcy Gregg, born in Columbia, and states rights activists Gist, Ellison Capers and J.S. Preston, all of whom are buried in Columbia.

During Reconstruction, the city was a focal point of attention, as South Carolina was one of the few states to have a black majority legislature, as well as a black attorney general, Robert Elliott; two black lieutenant governors, Alonzo Ransier and Richard Gleaves; and a member of the state supreme court, Jonathan Wright. In the disputed election of 1876, Columbia was a key player in both the struggle to end Reconstruction and to resolve the presidential election. In South Carolina, the 1876 election was rife with fraud on both sides. The Republicans counted the Democrats out and the Democrats ran a campaign of intimidation in both the gubernatorial and presidential races. The state was witness to the spectacle of two men claiming to be governor, the Democratic challenger General

Wade Hampton III of Civil War fame and the incumbent Republican Governor Daniel Chamberlain. Two general assemblies, known as the Wallace and Mackey Houses after the respective Speakers of each House, were battling it out as well. To save some room for actual ghost stories, the South Carolina Democrats gave in to Republican demands that they keep the White House in return for the end of Federal troops in the state and Federal noninterference in state elections, which spelled doom for the hopes of Republicans electing a governor for almost another one hundred years. Hampton and the Wallace House were duly recognized as the official state government and the redemption of the state was complete.

As the site of the state capital, Richland County is home to several educational institutions. These include the University of South Carolina, Columbia College, Allen University, Benedict College, Midlands Technical College, Lutheran Theological Southern Seminary and Columbia International University. Most, if not all, federal and state agencies are based out of Columbia due to its position as state capital and its central location in the state. All state governors since 1790 have lived in Columbia, though only three were born in Richland County—John Taylor, who also served as U.S. senator, James H. Adams and Duncan C. Heyward, who wrote *Seed from Madagascar*, which discussed rice planting in South Carolina. Wade Hampton III, who also served as both governor and U.S. senator, was born in Charleston but called Columbia home from 1838 until his death in 1902. James F. Byrnes, who served as U.S. senator, governor of South Carolina, U.S. secretary of state and as an associate justice of the U.S. Supreme Court, as well as in several New Deal–era federal positions, spent his latter years in Columbia and is buried at Trinity Episcopal Church Cemetery. As a small boy, U.S. President Woodrow Wilson lived in Columbia from 1870 to 1874 while his father served on the faculty of the Columbia Theological Seminary. The home he lived in is a National Historic Site and noted tourist attraction.

Other notable attractions in Richland County include Fort Jackson, the largest Initial Entry Training Center in the U.S. Army and the only military base located inside the city limits of its host city. Fort Jackson was named for the seventh president (and South Carolina native) Andrew Jackson. Columbia is also the only Southeastern city with direct access to three interstate highways, I-20, I-26 and I-77. Interstate 77's southern terminus is located near the Columbia Metropolitan Airport and the highway runs to Cleveland, Ohio. Near the community of Hopkins in the southern part of the county is South Carolina's only national park, Congaree National Park. Two other major attractions in the Columbia area are Riverbanks Zoo and Garden and the South Carolina State House grounds—home to some rather unique monuments, including the first monuments on the grounds of any state house dedicated to the contributions of African Americans to the state heritage. There is also a large monument in honor of the Confederacy, which regardless of one's politics is appropriate given South Carolina's role in Secession and the Civil War. Another interesting monument on the state house grounds is the grave of Captain Swanson Lunsford of Virginia, a veteran of the Revolution, which was the only grave on the grounds of a U.S. state capitol until the internment of U.S. Senator Huey Long at the new state capitol at Baton Rouge, Louisiana, in 1935.

Noted athletes with ties to the area include Kirby Higbe, a two-time All-Star pitcher in the 1940s with several teams, especially the Brooklyn Dodgers. Higbe was traded to the Pittsburgh Pirates in 1947 after refusing to play with Jackie Robinson, the first African American to play in the major leagues in the twentieth century. A National Basketball Association standout from the area, Alex English, was a longtime member of the Denver Nuggets and has been a member of the Basketball Hall of Fame since 1997. National Football League (NFL) players with ties to Richland County include George Rogers and Dan Reeves. George Rogers was winner of the 1980 Heisman Trophy and played for both the New Orleans Saints and Washington Redskins. He was a two-time NFL All-Pro and was a member of the Super Bowl XXII-winning Redskins squad. He is also a member of the College Football Hall of Fame. Dan Reeves, who played his entire career for the Dallas Cowboys and won one of the two Super Bowls he played, though none of the three he was involved in as a head coach, played quarterback for the University of South Carolina (USC). As a head coach, Reeves won three American Football Conference crowns with the Denver Broncos and one National Football Conference crown with the Atlanta Falcons. He also served as head coach for the New York Giants for three seasons and was the first opposing head coach to win a playoff game at famed Lambeau Field in Green Bay. He was also a two-time winner of the NFL Coach of the Year Award in 1993 and 1998.

Other coaches with ties to Richland County institutions include Bobby Cremins, who played basketball for USC before coaching at Georgia Tech and the College of Charleston, and Bobby Richardson, longtime baseball coach at USC, member of the New York Yankees dynasty in the 1950s and a native South Carolinian. Notable head football coaches at USC include Lou Holtz, Joe Morrison, Steve Spurrier and Jim Carlin. Frank McGuire, longtime head basketball coach at USC, was the only coach to take teams to both the Final Four of the Men's Basketball Tournament and to the College World Series (while at St. Johns). He also won the 1957 Men's Basketball NCAA Championship while at North Carolina before coming to USC. He is still the winningest men's basketball coach in school history. One other notable athlete from Richland County should be mentioned, though. Lillian Ellison, better known as the "Fabulous Moolah," was a longtime women's professional wrestling champion and was born in Columbia.

Notables from the arts with Richland County ties include director and choreographer Stanley Donen. Among Donen's other classic films, he is known for his work on *On the Town* (1949), with music by Leonard Bernstein, which he co-directed with Gene Kelly. This was the first movie musical to be filmed on location. Donen also directed *Royal Wedding* (1951), where he let Fred Astaire dance on the ceiling, and with Kelly again, Donen co-directed *Singin' in the Rain* (1952). Donen never won a competitive Academy Award over his long career, despite working with well-known stars and being known as the "King of the Hollywood musicals." He was awarded an honorary Oscar in 1998. Mary-Louise Parker, star of such films as *Fried Green Tomatoes* and *Boys on the Side* and television series including *The West Wing* and *Weeds*, was born at Fort Jackson. Noted muralist and sculptor Blue Sky, formerly known as Warren Johnson, works in Columbia. Two-time Grammy winning band Hootie and the Blowfish was formed by a group of then University of South Carolina students. This popular band followed about sixty years after Columbia's first big splash into pop culture. In the late 1930s, the dance known as the "Big Apple" arose from the nightclub of the same name in Columbia. The dance is similar to the Lindy Hop and the Shag and is a modified line dance. Tommy Dorsey recorded a song of the same title that sold well. It is one of the few dances that have been honored with a state historical marker. Kimberly Aiken, a Richland County resident, was named Miss America in 1993 and was the first black woman from the South to win the title.

Authors with Richland County ties include James Dickey, author of the novels *Deliverance* and *To the White Sea* and poet-in-residence at the University of South Carolina; Henry Timrod, known as the "Poet Laureate of the Confederacy," who lived in Columbia briefly at the end of the Civil War; and J. Gordon Coogler, father of the "cooglerism" typified by the famed couplet, "Alas, for the South! Her books have grown fewer/She never was much given to literature" and known for "poems written while you wait." His only published work *Purely Original Verse* was published in 1891 and is a hoot. I would be remiss if I failed to mention Columbia native T.F. Hamlin, winner of the 1956 Pulitzer Prize for biography for his work on architect Benjamin Latrobe.

Other fields in which folks with Richland County ties have excelled include law, education, religion and aviation. Notables in the legal field include Jean Toal, the first female justice and chief justice of the South Carolina Supreme Court and first native of Columbia to hold the position;

Matthew Perry, the first African American Federal Judge from the Deep South; and Isaac S.L. Johnson, one of the first African American graduates from the University of South Carolina Law School and one of the first African Americans to be elected to the South Carolina General Assembly as a Democrat. In the field of aviation, astronaut Charles F. Bolden Jr., veteran of four space shuttle missions, and Paul Redfern, pioneer aviator who was the first man to fly solo over the Caribbean and who made the first nonstop flight from North America to South America, are both Columbia natives. Paul Redfern was attempting to fly from Georgia to Rio de Janeiro when his plane apparently crashed somewhere in Venezuela in 1927. In the field of religion, Cardinal Joseph Bernardin, the Catholic Archbishop of Chicago from 1982 to his death in 1996, was born in Columbia. He was elevated to the College of Cardinals by Pope John Paul II in 1983.

SWAMP GIRL:
OLD STORY, NEW PLACE

The story of the vanishing hitchhiker has been around since the dawn of the automobile. Although it may vary slightly from place to place, the basics remain fairly constant. The story generally begins with a young and attractive lady, usually dressed in a dress that was stylish at least a generation ago, standing on the side of a quiet, once busy highway on a rainy or stormy night. A young man invariably stops and offers her a ride. The destination given by the young lady is always in one of the older residential neighborhoods in the nearest city of any size. The lady usually gets into the back seat and does not respond to repeated attempts at conversation. By the time the car arrives in the city's outskirts, the young man has to ask his passenger to repeat her destination. When he turns to ask, the back seat is empty, except for the jacket the man offered his passenger. The young man continues to his passenger's destination, only to discover that she had been killed in an accident years before at the same spot where she was picked up that night. Occasionally, the jacket leaves with the passenger and is retrieved from the young lady's headstone. This tale is probably America's most common ghost story. The only real competition it has is the ubiquitous "crybaby bridge." Many of these tales have a basis in fact but have grown into urban legends.

Due to its rural nature, South Carolina is home to more crybaby bridges than phantom hitchhikers, but the state does have a few. In my first book, I told the tale of Larry Stephens, the phantom pilot of S.C. Highway 107, and the ride I gave him. The tale of the "Swamp Girl of the Congaree" long predates that of Mr. Stephens and is found in collections of folklore gathered by the workers of the Works Progress Administration in the 1930s.

Our story begins with a young nursing student driving from Saint Matthews home to Columbia on U.S. Highway 601 in the late 1920s. Not having been around then, I cannot testify to the accuracy of the accounts, just the common elements. The night was stormy, cold and a bit foggy. As the young lady was crossing the Congaree River into Richland County, her car hit a slick spot and she lost control. The car caromed off both sides of the bridge, eventually slamming into the abutment on the Richland County side of the river. (The bridge is located just north of the junction of the Wateree and Congaree Rivers, above Lake Marion.) At some point, the young nurse-to-be was thrown from the car and into the river. A few days later, the car was recovered, but the body was not.

A few months later, a young couple was passing the same way in similar conditions when the wife spotted a figure on the roadside just after the bridge. Being a more innocent time, the couple stopped and offered assistance. The young lady requested a ride to an address on Pickens Street in downtown Columbia to see her ill mother. When asked how she came to be standing beside such a remote stretch of road, the young nurse, who was in a muddy uniform, mumbled something about car trouble. The young couple could not recall seeing any abandoned vehicles, but simply assumed they had been focused on watching the road in such nasty weather. The wife tried to make small talk on the drive into downtown, but the passenger did not respond. As the car began encountering traffic, the husband glanced back to enquire about the best route to take when he nearly wrecked the car. The back seat was empty, save for a small muddy puddle behind his wife. The doors were still locked and the windows were up, but no passenger was present. The wife became very upset, as did the husband. However, a desire for answers led the couple to continue to Pickens Street to determine the tale behind their strange encounter. The mother, of course, had been dead for weeks and the family stated that the couple had not been the first to pick up the young nurse, who was still trying to see her mother. Other odd events have been recorded in the area of Bluff Road (S.C. Highway 48). Notable among these are a horse-drawn carriage that races with cars, figures seen in the swamps and a bridge where cars are prone to stall out. I have not yet run across any of these occurrences, but if I do, I'll let you know.

My encounters with the Swamp Girl have been very similar to the one described above. My first encounter occurred on a stormy autumn night in the late 1980s. As I have mentioned before, I am a huge fan of so-called "short cuts" and back roads. While returning to Lyman from a weekend in Charleston, I encountered an accident on I-26 near Orangeburg. To avoid the traffic, I decided to take U.S. 601 to S.C. 48 to I-77 in order to get to Columbia and get back on I-26. At no point did I expect to have an encounter with anything out of the ordinary, as it was already late and I am not overly fond of deer on back roads in the rain. Shortly after crossing the Congaree River, but before I turned onto S.C. 48, I saw a rather attractive young lady in an old-fashioned nurse's outfit standing on the shoulder of the road. Thinking that the girl had been to a costume party and recalling that I had seen just one other car since leaving the interstate, I decided to give her a ride to the nearest pay phone as my good deed for the year.

I stopped about ten yards from her and she walked to the car. As I opened the back door to let her in, I saw that the starched white skirt was soaked and very muddy. She explained that she had had some car trouble and asked for a ride to Pickens Street in Columbia. She also asked if she could lie down and rest in the back since she had put in a long night at work. I said sure and off we went. After I crossed under I-77, I remembered that I did not have a map of Columbia with me and turned to wake her and get directions. Imagine my nineteen-year-old reaction to an empty backseat. Well, empty except for a puddle of smelly rainwater and thick mud across the fabric. After I stopped at the next gas station and calmed down, I remembered where I had picked her up. I decided not to add my name to the lengthy list of folks who had disturbed her family and continued on my way.

My second encounter was merely in passing. My wife Rachel and I were en route to see some friends in Charleston when we heard about a major accident at the junction of I-77 and I-26. Naturally, I decided to avoid traffic and headed down Bluff Road toward U.S. 601. Just after we got off the interstate, the long-threatening clouds burst. Shortly after we passed the entrance to what was then the Congaree Swamp National Monument, I mentioned my last trip down Bluff Road to my wife. Naturally, she blasted me for picking up a hitchhiker and doubted my honesty! After a few minutes of chat about such things and several good-natured (I hope) questions about my common sense, the topic died off as my attention returned to watching the wet, winding road and looking out for deer. Just after we turned onto U.S. 601, my wife gasped. I asked what was wrong and she said nothing. On reaching the interstate, I stopped to grab some much needed caffeine and decided to find out what had upset my wife. She told me that she had seen a figure in a white dress walking down the grassy shoulder of the road. As we passed the figure, Rachel said she could see the trees through the figure, hence the gasp. I was very much determined to go back when Rachel informed me that I would have to choose between a loving and happy wife and a long dead nurse. I made the right decision, as Rachel and I are still married.

FORT JACKSON: MORE THAN JUST INFANTRY TRAINING?

Fort Jackson has been a key part of the midlands of South Carolina since its opening in 1917 as an artillery training camp. It was named after Andrew Jackson, the only native of South Carolina to be elected president, who was born in modern Lancaster County. Camp Jackson's first recruits arrived in September 1917 and thousands of trainees passed the gates before the end of World War I in 1918. The camp was reactivated in 1940 after the passage of the Selective Service Act to serve as a basic training center. Several well-known infantry divisions received training at the base before being deployed overseas in World War II and all following conflicts. These divisions are recognized with state historical highway markers on the base. Fort Jackson was annexed by the city of Columbia in 1968 with the blessing of the Pentagon. It is the major entry point into the U.S. Army for women.

However, there is another side to Fort Jackson. Two areas on the base seem to be especially active spots for paranormal encounters. The artillery range is known for sightings of a female soldier in full battle gear with a gaping hole in her helmet. The theory behind her return is that she committed suicide in one of the nearby latrines. How the hole got in her helmet if she was a suicide is a question unanswered by my sources. I mean, most suicides don't wear protective gear, and since neither the Public Affairs Office or the Fort Jackson museum have any information on any hauntings on base, I guess I'll have to wait until I can visit and hopefully see for myself.

The other haunting at Fort Jackson is centered in the B Company Barracks (369th AG). Online accounts mention a feeling of being watched while in the dayroom at all hours. The black shadow of a man (believed to be a sergeant) has been seen walking to the door of each room and then entering a restroom. The figure is seen opening the door and closing himself in, but is not found in the bathroom. To my knowledge, he has not been seen in any other rooms. As mentioned above, the Public Affairs Office has no confirmed reports of any hauntings on base and told me that the base personnel have more important things to worry about. I have to agree with them on that, what with two wars currently being fought and all. I plan to get down to the base and play with both the gentleman in the barracks and the woman with the hole in her helmet at some point. If there is a second edition of this book, I will try to get more information and more eyewitness accounts.

BLANDING STREET SEEMS TO ATTRACT THE "ONE-AND-DONES"

What I call "one-and-dones" are better known to students of ghost lore as crisis apparitions. Crisis apparitions are ghost that have minimal interaction with the living and usually appear to serve as a warning of future events or to protect a site from interference of one kind or another. Blanding Street is a major east-west route through downtown Columbia and has been the site of two such occurrences. The earliest recorded event was at the site of the former Christ Episcopal Church at the corner of Marion and Blanding Streets. The church burned in February 1865 along with much of Columbia's antebellum architecture. For several months after the fire, neighbors and passersby reported seeing "angels" gathering the shell of the chancel at the spot formerly occupied by the altar. I believe that the "angels" were returning Confederate veterans who meant for no further harm to come to the building. However, more sinister motives could be attributed to the figures, such as looters or other criminals taking advantage of the credulity of a beaten and demoralized populace. The church did not recover from this trauma and by 1870 the parish was defunct.

The second appearance dates to the spring of 1914 and is much better documented than the "angels" at Christ Episcopal. The apparition of a phantom on horseback above the treetops appeared nightly for about a week and caused quite the sensation. The figure was seen to appear, then the horse reared and took off on a journey of unknown purpose. Despite the detail visible in the figure, including the stitching on the saddle and reins, exactly who it was is still the source of some controversy. Contemporary accounts claim that it was one of the Four Horsemen of the Apocalypse or that it was former Confederate General Wade Hampton III. The appearance of Hampton was mentioned in connection with the start of World War I that autumn, as a forewarning of the bloodshed to come. To my ears, this sounds like a posthumous explanation that no one thought of at the time. Since General Hampton had been dead for twelve years at this point, I doubt he would be very concerned with the outbreak of a war in Europe. Sadly, I must write this off using the time-honored excuse of "mass hysteria." I think that once the word got out about the phantom horseman, the story grew from there and folks saw what they wanted to see.

SALUDA COUNTY

S aluda County was formed by the State Constitutional Convention of
1895 from Edgefield County. The name of the county was the source
of a rift between U.S. Senator Benjamin Tillman and his brother George.
George Tillman favored naming the county after the Butler family, which
gave the state several governors, senators and other leaders, while Ben was
politically opposed to the family and preferred the name Saluda, the name of
an Indian tribe once located in the area and the river that flows through the
state. The name Saluda means river of corn. Since Ben Tillman controlled
the convention, the name Saluda was chosen. Saluda County is the only
South Carolina County not formed and organized by the legislature. It
is bounded by Greenwood, Edgefield, Aiken, Lexington and Newberry
Counties. Native American influence in the area dates back to about 1000
BC with the Cherokee and Saluda tribes. The former Cherokee village of
Saluda Old Town was the site of a treaty between the Cherokee and the
British in 1755. The county suffered several raids during the Cherokee
War of 1760–61. The only South Carolina governor from Saluda county
was Pierce M. Butler, who served his state not only as governor but also as
commander of the Palmetto Regiment during the Mexican War where he
lost his life at the Battle of Churubusco. Two defenders of the Alamo, William
Barnett Travis and James Bonham (the older brother of Governor Milledge
Bonham) were native sons of Saluda County, as well as second cousins. (We'll
tell their story shortly.) Saluda County was the site of one Revolutionary
War armed encounter. There are no recorded Civil War incidents in
the county. As yet, no U.S. senators have hailed from Saluda County.

BACK TO SOUTH TEXAS

As mentioned above, two of the defenders of the Alamo in San Antonio, Texas, were natives of Saluda County, second cousins William Barnett Travis and James Bonham. No sites connected with William B. Travis are still standing in Saluda County today with the possible exception of Red Bank Baptist Church, where both men's families are known to have worshipped. James Bonham's legacy in the county is marked by two of his family's homes, a family cemetery and his younger brother's service to his state. For those readers who may not be acquainted with the Alamo, here's a brief recap of the events to set the stage for the rest of our tale.

The siege at the Alamo had its roots in the desire of the Mexican government to control its borders and regulate its internal affairs, especially in the fast growing province of Texas. An influx of American, mainly Southern, settlers had swollen the population faster than the Mexican authorities could maintain order. The fact that the Mexican Constitution had ended slavery also threatened the economic interests of the American settlers. Strangely, many Mexicans in Texas supported the revolt, sharing their American neighbors' beliefs in states rights over the claims of Mexican President Santa Anna that the central government should be supreme. Santa Anna's main focus was on ending the rebellion and restoring the rule of the central government. The Texans were in favor of either independence or joining the United States.

The lines had been drawn when Santa Anna arrived outside the walls of the mission on February 23, 1836, with about 6,000 men and twenty cannons. The defenders' forces totaled about 250 with only a few cannons. (Considering that number, I wonder what the odds of victory were.) The siege lasted thirteen days with the final assault planned for March 6, 1836. Lieutenant Colonel William B. Travis had taken command of the post on February 3, 1836, following a brief dispute with Jim Bowie over who could parley with the Mexican army. In the end, the parley talks failed and Bowie's health steadily worsened over the course of the siege. Lieutenant Colonel Travis sent his fellow Saluda County native and second cousin, James Bonham, to the nearby garrison at Goliad to request assistance. Bonham returned with a promise of some 300 men on the way, but a lack of transportation caused the attempt to fail. (The garrison at Goliad was massacred following its surrender after the fall of the Alamo.) Prior to this, according to legend, Colonel Travis drew a line in the sand in the courtyard and ordered those who would die for Texan independence to step over it. All but one defender did so, even if Jim Bowie had to be carried over it in his sickbed. The tale is not confirmed, but the phrase "a line in the sand" has won Travis immortality beyond military circles.

The siege of the Alamo was professionally conducted with bands blaring all night, sporadic cannon fire and the steady approach of some 1,600 men toward the walls. A blood red flag was raised by the attackers and the bugle call "El Deguello," which meant roughly "no quarter asked or given," echoed through the dawn. The attackers had to cross about one thousand yards of open ground to reach the walls, which helps explain the high casualty rate suffered by the Mexican army. William B. Travis fell early in the battle, at the first breach in the wall, of a gunshot wound to the head. In just over an hour, the Mexican army had killed every defender and freed about two dozen slaves, women and children. The bodies of the slain defenders were burned as a warning to other rebels and to signify that there would be no martyrdom for the insurgents. On April 21, 1836, the garrisons at the Alamo and at Goliad would be avenged when the Texan army under General Sam Houston defeated Santa Anna at San Jacinto. In order to ensure his release, Santa Anna ordered the remaining Mexican troops in Texas to return to Mexico and Texas formally was lost to Mexican control. Total Mexican losses were high, totaling about 600 killed and/or wounded out of 1,600 engaged. The defense of the Alamo is now recognized around the world as an example of American heroism.

The haunting at the Alamo dates to the end of April 1836, when the retreating Mexican troops were ordered to tear down the Alamo as revenge for their defeat and to honor their losses in the siege. I'm sure spiting the victorious Texans may have played a role as well. In any case, a detachment of Mexican engineers were ordered to tear down the adobe walls of the old mission and to blow up the old chapel inside the walls. The Mexicans were confronted by a group of men armed with flaming swords who denied the terrified men entry to the building. On reporting this event to their commander, General Andrade, he went to the building and met with the same circumstances. At least one version of this tale names the six men as Colonel Travis, Jim Bowie, Davy Crockett, James Bonham, Captain John W. Smith and Isaac Millsaps. Other reports credit hands that emerged from the walls of the building, some carrying torches, with dissuading the Mexican engineers. A booming voice that threatened a horrible death to anyone who damaged the building could have been a practical joker, but it's rather difficult to fake arms emerging from sun-dried mud bricks. In any case, the building was left as it was.

In the late 1890s, parts of the interior were to be removed as an early urban renewal campaign. This riled up the guardian spirits again. Men were seen walking on the walls and moans and whispers were heard as well. The clanking of chains also echoed inside the walls. Franciscan monks had constructed the building in the 1700s, and the clanking of the chains was blamed on those who had forgotten their vows and had been imprisoned in the old mission.

Cold spots and strange noises have been reported in the museum onsite, located in the long barracks where some of the fiercest hand-to-hand combat occurred. From the sites of the three funeral pyres come reports of a strong smell of wood smoke, light going on and off, small items moving unassisted and cold spots. The pyres have been tentatively located on the site of a fire station on Houston Street, near a former boarding house on East Commerce Street and on the site of the River Center Mall. All of these locations are in the city limits of modern San Antonio.

I have not had an opportunity as yet to visit San Antonio. When I do, I will be sure to visit this shrine to Texan heroism and one of the most haunted spots in America. According to several sources, figures are still seen on the walls and the museum still receives complaints about odd noises and cold spots, especially on the anniversary of the final assault.

BIBLIOGRAPHY

ARTICLES

Aiken (SC) Standard and Review, July 6, 1965.

Barker, Carol. "Ghosts or Psychic Energy?" *Orangeburg (SC) Times and Democrat*, October 18, 2002.

Gilliland, Betsy. "Hotel Has Been Central to Social Scene." *Augusta (GA) Chronicle*, September 13, 2005.

NeSmith, Sandy. "Redcliffe the Perfect Place for a Haunting." *Aiken (SC) Standard*, October 30, 2000.

Patterson, Lezlie. "Ghost Town." *Columbia (SC) State*, July 22, 2006.

Still, Lisa. "Creaks, Groans and Things That Go Bump in the Night: Story Two." *Barnwell (SC) People-Sentinel*, May 26, 2005.

Wells, Monica. "Midland Valley Maiden." *Aiken (SC) Standard*, October 30, 2001.

Wood, Marjorie. "Aiken's Ghosts Exposed During Tour." *Aiken (SC) Standard*, April 5, 2005.

Books

Barefoot, Daniel. *Touring South Carolina's Revolutionary War Sites.* Winston-Salem, NC: John F. Blair, Publisher, 1999.

Barrett, John. *Sherman's March through the Carolinas.* Chapel Hill: University of North Carolina Press, 1956.

Bierer, Bert, ed. *South Carolina Indian Lore.* Columbia, SC: State Printing Company, 1972.

Boyanski, John. *Ghosts of Upstate South Carolina.* Mountville, PA: Shelor and Son Publishing, 2006.

Boylston, Raymond. *Healing Springs: A History of the Springs and the Surrounding Area.* Orangeburg, SC: Sandlapper Publishing Company, 2004.

Brimelow, Judith, ed. *South Carolina Highway Historical Marker Guide.* Columbia: South Carolina Department of Archives and History, 1992.

Brockington, William, Jr. *Historic Sketches on Aiken: A Collection of the Best of 150 Years of Our Southern City.* Aiken, SC, 1985.

Chapman, John. *History of Edgefield County from the Earliest Settlements to 1897.* Newberry, SC: Hubert Aull, Printer and Publisher, 1897.

Clarke, Philip, Jr. *A Visitor's Guide to Historic Abbeville, South Carolina.* Abbeville, SC: Commercial Printing Company, 1970.

Davis, Burke. *Sherman's March.* New York: Random House, 1980.

Edgar, Walter, ed. *The South Carolina Encyclopedia.* Columbia: University of South Carolina Press, 2006.

Edmonds, Bobby. *The Making of McCormick County.* McCormick, SC: Cedar Hill Unlimited, 1999.

Encyclopedia of South Carolina: A Volume of the Encyclopedia of the United States. New York: Somerset, 1993.

Floyd, E. Randall. *Great Southern Mysteries.* New York: Barnes and Noble Books, 2000.

———. *In the Realm of Ghosts and Hauntings: 40 Supernatural Occurrences from Around the World.* New York: Barnes and Noble Books, 2002.

Freeman, Douglas Southall. *R.E. Lee: A Biography.* Vol. 4. New York: Charles Scribner's Sons, 1935.

Gibbes, Colonel James G. *Who Burnt Columbia?* Newberry, SC: Elbert H. Aull, 1902.

Graydon, Nell, comp. *South Carolina Ghost Stories.* Beaufort, SC: Beaufort BookShop, Inc., 1969.

Graydon, Nell. *Tales of Columbia.* Columbia, SC: R.L. Bryan, 1964.

Grier, Ralph. *Legends of Erskine College.* N.p., n.d. From the Collections of McCain Library, Erskine College, Due West, SC.

Guiley, Rosemary Ellen. *The Encyclopedia of Ghosts and Spirits.* 2nd ed. New York: Checkmark Books, 2000.

Haining, Peter. *A Dictionary of Ghost Lore.* Englewood Cliffs, NJ: Prentice-Hall, 1984.

Hauck, Dennis William. *Haunted Places: The National Directory; Ghostly Abodes, Sacred Sites, UFO Landings, and Other Supernatural Locations.* New York: Penguin, 2002.

Hennig, Helen Kohn, ed. *Columbia: Capital City of South Carolina, 1786–1936.* Columbia, SC: R.L. Bryan, 1936. Authorized by the Columbia Sesquicentennial Commission.

Hilborn, Nat, and Sam Hilborn. *Battleground of Freedom: South Carolina in the Revolution.* Columbia, SC: Sandlapper Publishing, 1970.

Ivers, Larry. *Colonial Forts of South Carolina, 1670–1775.* Columbia: University of South Carolina Press, 1970.

BIBLIOGRAPHY

Johnson, Clint. *Touring the Carolinas' Civil War Sites.* Winston-Salem, NC: John F. Blair, Publisher, 1996

Julien, Carl. *Beneath So Kind A Sky: The Scenic and Architectural Beauty of South Carolina.* Columbia: University of South Carolina Press, 1947.

————. *Ninety Six: Landmarks of South Carolina's Last Frontier Region.* Columbia: University of South Carolina Press, 1950.

————. *Sea Islands to Sand Hills.* Columbia: University of South Carolina Press, 1954.

Lawton, Alexania, and Minnie Wilson. *Allendale on the Savannah.* Bamberg, SC: Bamberg Herald Printers, 1970.

Lipscomb, Terry. *Battles, Skirmishes, and Actions of the American Revolution in South Carolina.* Columbia: South Carolina Department of Archives and History, 1991.

McNeil, W.K., ed. *Ghost Stories from the American South.* Little Rock: August House, 1985.

Milliken, Helen. *Behind the Scenes: Sketches of Selected South Carolina First Ladies.* Spartanburg, SC: Heritage Information Fund Press, 2001.

Murphy, Jim. *Inside the Alamo.* New York: Delacorte, 2003.

Neuffer, Claude, and Irene Neuffer. *Correct Mispronunciations of Some South Carolina Names.* 5th ed. Columbia: University of South Carolina Press, 1991.

Rhyne, Nancy, ed. *Slave Ghost Stories: Tales of Hags, Hants, Ghosts, and Diamondback Rattlers.* Orangeburg, SC: Sandlapper Publishing, 2002.

Roberts, Nancy. *Ghosts of the Carolinas.* 2nd ed. Charlotte, NC: McNally and Loftin, Publishers, 1967.

————. *South Carolina Ghosts from the Coast to the Mountains.* Columbia: University of South Carolina Press, 1983.

BIBLIOGRAPHY

Saluda County Tricentennial Commission. *Saluda County in Scene and Story.* Columbia, SC: R.L. Bryan, 1970.

Simons, Jane Kealhofer. *A Guide to Columbia, South Carolina's Capital City.* Columbia, SC: R.L. Bryan, 1945.

South Carolina: A Guide to the Palmetto State. New York: Oxford University Press, 1941.

South Carolina Biographical Dictionary. New York: Somerset, 1994.

Stauffer, Michael. *The Formation of Counties in South Carolina.* Columbia: South Carolina Department of Archives and History, 1994.

Summer, G. Leland. *Folklore of South Carolina, Including Central and Dutch Fork Section Of the State, and Much Data on the Early Quaker and Covenanter Customs, Etc.* N.p., n.d. Copy in S. Lewis Bell Room Collection, Chester County Library.

Thalimer, Dan, and Carol Thalimer. *Country Roads of South Carolina.* Lincolnwood, IL: Country Roads Press, 1999.

Todd, Carolina, and Sidney Wait. *South Carolina, a Day at a Time.* Orangeburg, SC: Sandlapper Publishing, 1998.

Toney, B. Keith. *Battlefield Ghosts.* Berryville, VA: Rockbridge Publishing, 1997.

Turnage, Shelia. *Haunted Inns of the Southeast.* Winston-Salem, NC: John F. Blair, 2001.

Vexler, Robert, ed. *Chronology and Documentary Handbook of the State of South Carolina.* William Swindler, series ed. Dobbs Ferry, NY: Oceana, 1978.

Watson, Margaret. *Greenwood County Sketches: Old Roads and Early Settlers.* Greenwood, SC: Attic Press, 1970.

Williams, Docia, and Reneta Byrne. *Spirits of San Antonio and South Texas.* Plano, TX: Wordware Publishing, 1993.

Woody, Howard, and Thomas L. Johnson. *Postcard History Series: South Carolina Postcards Volume Three West Central Carolina Aiken to Saluda.* Charleston, SC: Arcadia Publishing, 2001.

Workers of the Writers' Program of the Works Progress Administration in the State of South Carolina. *Palmetto Place Names: Their Origins and Meanings.* Columbia: South Carolina Educational Association, n.d.

PERSONAL INTERVIEWS

Cope, Kim. Owner, Cedar Grove Plantation, Hampton County, SC. E-mail exchange with author. January 24, 2005.

Freeman, Charlie. Owner, Abbewood Bed and Breakfast, Abbeville County, SC. Telephone interview. September 18, 2006.

Genevie, Michael. Director, Abbeville Opera House. Telephone interview. September 16, 2006.

Martin, Marie. Director, Voorhees College Library, Bamberg County, SC. Personal interview. August 10, 2006.

Peterson, Alan. Owner, Belmont Inn, Abbeville County, SC. Telephone interview. September 18, 2006.

Phillips, Robin. Volunteer, Calhoun County Cares. Personal interview. August 19, 2006.

Standridge, Sheri. Director, Abbeville Chamber of Commerce. Telephone interview. September 18, 2006.

Tisdale, Dr. Henry. President, Claflin University, Orangeburg County, SC. Personal interview. August 18, 2006.

Williams, Diana. Manager, Rosemary Hall, Aiken County, SC. Telephone interview. September 18, 2006.

BIBLIOGRAPHY

WEBSITES

Local Legend: The Reverend J. Brown Gordon Coogler (1865–1901). http://www.blythewoodnet.net/np-j-gordon-coogler.htm.

The Shadowlands, Ghosts and Hauntings. http://theshadowlands.net/ places/southcarolina.htm/.

Southern Ghost Stories. http://southcarolinaghost.tripod.com/ GhostStories/.

ABOUT THE AUTHOR

T ally Johnson has been fascinated by the rich ghost lore of his native South Carolina for over twenty-five years. Born in Spartanburg into a family of readers, his interest in ghost stories was first piqued by a presentation by author and storyteller Nancy Roberts to his fifth grade class at Lyman Elementary. As he got older, he visited many reputedly haunted sites throughout the Carolinas and Georgia and had enough encounters with various manifestations to convince him that ghosts do exist. Johnson, who has a library of over one hundred books of ghost stories, noticed that the ghost lore of inland South Carolina has been neglected for too long.

Mr. Johnson is a graduate of Spartanburg Methodist College and Wofford College with degrees in history from both institutions. Following work toward his MA in history at Winthrop University, which he just missed completing before real life intervened, he became local history coordinator at the Chester County Library. As part of his outreach to local schools, and in response to repeated prodding by his wife Rachel, he began telling students about his experiences with ghosts. After

Photo by Jonathan Phillips.

many complaints about poor writing and a lack of local lore in the books of ghost lore he bought, his friends challenged him to write a book that would meet his standards. *Ghosts of the South Carolina Upcountry*, his first book for The History Press, was the result.

Mr. Johnson currently serves as branch manager for the Great Falls branch of the Chester County Library and is active in many community groups, including Chester County First Steps, the Clemson Extension Advisory Board for Chester County and the Chester Little Theater, among others. He is on the South Carolina Arts Commission's Roster of Approved Artists and the South Carolina School Librarians list of storytellers. He is also a past member of the Palmetto Archives, Libraries, and Museums Council on Preservation (PALMCOP), Phi Alpha Theta (the graduate history honor society) and the South Carolina Storytellers Association. He enjoys spending time with his family and friends, hiking, visiting historic sites and reading.

Please visit us at
www.historypress.net